Another favorite book from
my favorite stitchin...

Merry Christmas —

Sue

1997

MILNER CRAFT SERIES

Embroider A Garden

DIANA LAMPE

SALLY MILNER PUBLISHING

First published in 1993 by
Sally Milner Publishing Pty Ltd
558 Darling Street
Rozelle NSW 2039 Australia

Reprinted 1993, 1994, 1995 (twice)

© Embroidery design, artwork and text, Diana Lampe 1993

Design by Gatya Kelly, Doric Order
Photography by Matt Kelso
Stitch illustrations by Don Bradford
Flower illustrations by Diana Lampe
Typeset in Australia by Asset Typesetting Pty Ltd
Printed in Australia by Impact Printing, Melbourne

National Library of Australia
Cataloguing-in-Publication data:

Lampe, Diana.
    [More embroidered garden flowers]. Embroider a garden

    [U.S. ed.]
    ISBN 1 86351 122 9

    1. Embroidery — Patterns. 2. Decoration and ornament —
    Plant forms. I. Title. II. Title : More embroidered garden
    flowers. (Series : Milner craft series).

746.44041

I dedicate this book to my mother
May Sarah Lampe
who encouraged me from early childhood to explore my creativity

Diana Lampe, 1993

ACKNOWLEDGEMENTS

Writing, illustrating and completing the embroidery for this book has been a long and often difficult task. It has been made very much easier by the enthusiastic interest and encouragement of my family and many friends and students who have been looking forward to this publication. I would like to express my special gratitude to a number of people.

I wish to thank David Harper for his continuing support and advice. I have relied on, and been guided by, his knowledge of the English language while writing the text of this book.

Love and appreciation to Charlotte, Sophie and Nicholas who have had to adjust to my new lifestyle and have coped in a mature way with a mother who is often travelling, distracted and disorganised.

This book is a companion volume to *Embroidered Garden Flowers* which Jane Fisk and I worked on together. That experience has made the writing of this book very much easier, and I express my appreciation for having worked with Jane and learned much from her.

Many thanks to Paddy and Jack Hornsby of Affinity Plus, with whom I have worked very closely for several years.

On the domestic scene, I would like to thank Krystyna Koltun for helping to keep my house in order and Keith Alden, who for many years has cheerfully tended and helped create my gardens — the source of much inspiration.

I have had a team of helpers whom I wish to thank most sincerely for their part in *More Embroidered Garden Flowers*. They are:

Gillian Falvey, who has embroidered all my gardens and has been of invaluable help in preparing the text. She has spent a great deal of time working through the book with me, helping with the difficult task of expressing the technical aspects of the embroidery in a clear and concise way.

Geoffrey Brooks, who has spent many hours setting up my computer and helping me to use it, and has always been available to assist me.

Dianne Firth, for botanical advice, and Maggie Taylor for embroidering a beautiful cushion especially for this book.

Irene Ussenko and Gail Lubbock, for help with typing, and Thea Maclean for some excellent editing.

Sally Milner and staff, for bringing the book together.

Matt Kelso, for the time and effort which he has put into the photography.

Don Bradford, for the clear stitch illustrations.

Ross Henty, for allowing me to use his helpful notes on the framing of needlework.

I wish to thank Dollfus-Mieg & Cie — Paris, for granting permission to use the DMC© trademark throughout this book, and for donating the threads used in the designs.

Finally, my appreciation to the needlework shops around Australia which have promoted my work. I have had the opportunity to visit quite a number of these and to give classes. As a result I have made many new friends.

Diana Lampe, 1993

CONTENTS

INTRODUCTION

This book is the companion volume to *Embroidered Garden Flowers* which was enthusiastically received by embroiderers and garden lovers alike. The response was so overwhelming that I have been encouraged to put more of my flowers and gardens into this second book. These additional flowers will greatly expand your embroidery repertoire.

I have a considerable love of gardens; I've established several over the years and grown all the flowers in these two books. After being introduced to my embroidery, many people have become interested in carefully studying flowers and have become keen gardeners themselves.

I started embroidering flower gardens seven years ago and it has totally changed my life. Maybe this will happen to you, too! I hope that many of the people who enjoyed the first book and completed a Spring Garden will now complete the four seasons and derive as much pleasure as I do from having the set hanging in their homes.

The individual flowers described in the Flower Glossary can be used for many other purposes. Work them in any appropriate size or whatever medium you wish; silk or wool, for example. Adorn clothing and gifts with flowers to create attractive individual items. Included in the colour plates is an exquisite silk cushion, embroidered by my friend Maggie Taylor, which uses a range of my flowers.

I have included instructions for the passionflower in the Flower Glossary although it does not appear in any of the gardens. Despite its complexity, it is the favourite among my students. Although not suitable for the Summer Garden because of its scale, it would look lovely in the Summer Garland.

My aim in writing this book has been to document my designs. I have spent so many years thinking about and devising ways to depict flowers realistically in needlework I feel that it would be a great shame if they were not shared and recorded to give pleasure to many.

I hope I have achieved my aim and produced a book that is user-friendly with clear and precise instructions. Take a little time to look through the pages and familiarise yourself with the layout before you start work. You shouldn't have any trouble finding your way around. Consult the index and you'll quickly find the flower or stitch you need.

The opening chapter gives general information on the materials and tools required. The following chapters give descriptions of the Summer, Autumn and Winter Gardens and the Summer Garland and include working notes and lists of flowers and prerequisites. 'Finishing Touches' sets out in detail how to wash and press your finished piece and also information on framing.

The following chapters give descriptions of the Summer, Autumn and Winter Gardens and the Summer Garland and include working notes and lists of flowers and prerequisites.

The Flower Glossary gives specific instructions and illustrations for the individual flowers. The flowers are featured in alphabetical order, with the garden ornaments and insects at the end.

Instructions and illustrations for all the stitches needed to work the flowers in this book are given in the Stitch Glossary. Left-handed embroiderers have not been forgotten; the illustrations have been reproduced in mirror-image.

Finally, in the appendices are some notes by Ross Henty: 'The Framing of Needlework'; and a list of DMC stranded cottons in numerical order with colour names as a reference.

An embroidered sampler of each season, in actual size, is included in the colour plates. Refer to these samplers while working on the flowers to help you with their relative scale.

Now it's time to begin. Find a pleasant, well-lit place to sit, arrange everything you need in front of you, and start stitching. I always listen to some beautiful music while working — what an enjoyable and satisfying way to spend one's time. If you are not a very experienced embroiderer, don't be daunted. Take it one step at a time and you'll be rewarded by the beauty of your finished piece.

Diana Lampe, 1993

CHAPTER 1

BEFORE YOU BEGIN

O lady, leave thy silken thread
  And flowery tapestrie:
There's living roses on the bush,
  And blossoms on the tree;
Stoop where thou wilt, thy careless hand
  Some random bud will meet;
Thou canst not tread, but thou wilt find
  The daisy at thy feet.

Thomas Hood

NEEDLES

Embroidery crewel needles are used for most stitches because the length of the shaft and the large eye make them easy to work with. However, a straw or millinery needle should always be used when working bullion stitch and lazy daisy bullion stitch because the long shaft and small eye will pass through the wraps easily, resulting in an even stitch.

To avoid confusion, I have noted the appropriate needle to use for each step in the Flower Glossary, but to summarise, use:

- No 7 crewel or straw needle for three to four strands of thread.
- No 8 crewel or straw needle for two strands of thread.
- No 9 crewel or straw needle for one strand of thread.

THREADS

DMC stranded cotton (embroidery floss) has been used for the designs in this book. It is a lustrous, six-stranded thread which can be separated into the required number of strands. It is readily available and comes in a wide range of colours.

USE OF THREADS

The correct end of the thread to pull from the skein should be obvious. Note also the illustration on the paper band. Don't cut your thread too long. The best length with which to sew is approximately 40 cm (16″). This is about the distance from your fingertips to your elbow.

It is important to *strip* the thread before embroidering in order to aerate the strands and ensure smooth coverage when the stitches are worked. This means separating all the individual strands of your cut thread, and then putting back together the number of individual strands you require. When separating your strands, hold the thread at the top and pull the individual strands upwards to avoid tangling.

All spun threads should be worked with the grain. This is important because the thread will twist and unravel if worked against it. Run your fingers down the thread to feel the grain; smooth is with the grain, rough is against it.

To ensure you use the thread in the correct direction, always thread the needle with the 'blooming end'. This is the end you pull from the DMC skein. If you are unsure which is correct, flick or rub the ends and the right one will 'bloom'. If your thread has been resting for a while the 'blooming end' will have become untwisted and fluffy.

FABRIC

In my experience, the best fabric to work with is Irish embroidery linen. It is firm and will last longer than most other fabrics. Silk or unbleached calico can also be used for a pleasing effect.

SCISSORS

A small pair of good quality embroidery scissors with sharp, pointed blades is needed for snipping your threads.

PENCILS

A soft lead pencil (such as 2B) should be used in preference to any other marker. This is because some marking pencils leave chemical residues in the fabric which can ultimately reappear or rot the fabric. Pencil marks are easily removed by washing your finished embroidery. If you wish to change the pencilled outline while you are working, remove it by gentle rubbing with an Artgum eraser or stale bread.

HOOPS

For good tension, I recommend the use of a small embroidery hoop for couching, French knot stalks and all stitches of the satin stitch family. Also, when working French knots and colonial knots, you will have more control, and be able to develop a rhythm, if a small 10 cm (4″) hoop is used.

A plastic hoop is smooth and good to use. Traditional wooden hoops are also satisfactory but should be wrapped with white cotton tape to avoid damaging your work.

CHAPTER 2

NOTES FOR EMBROIDERED GARDENS

Winter is cold-hearted,
*   Spring is yea and nay,*
Autumn is a weathercock
*   Blown every way:*
Summer days for me
When every leaf is on its tree.

Christina Rossetti

The size you wish your finished embroidered garden to be is very much up to you. If it is to be larger than mine, be sure you use a piece of linen large enough to ensure ample fabric around your finished embroidery for framing.

If you plan to work more than one garden and to hang them together, take care to make them all the same size. Consider the balance of colour, density and form and how they will look when hanging together on your wall.

You may choose to arrange the flowers in your garden differently to mine, making some clumps larger, or including a few of your own flower ideas. You might copy an ornamental feature from your garden, or include your own pet, a bird or an insect. Challenge your creativity and I am sure you'll be well satisfied with the result.

The following detailed instructions on the order in which to work your embroidered garden are given simply to guide those of you who are not yet confident enough to design your own garden. Read through the chapter on your chosen project, look carefully at the garden and flower illustrations, turn to the Flower Glossary and start stitching. Let your garden grow as mine does — freely from the needle and thread.

Included in each of the following garden chapters is a list of flowers and other inclusions, as well as prerequisites for each project.

CHAPTER 3

THE SUMMER GARDEN

Come honey-bee, with thy busy hum,
To the fragrant tufts of wild thyme come,
And sip the sweet dew from the cowslip's head,
From the lily's bell and the violet's bed.

Anon.

A sundial is at the centre of my Summer Garden. It is surrounded by a riot of colour: stately sunflowers, agapanthus, cheerful shasta daisies, rose campion and evening primrose, homely chamomile and heartsease. Elegant gardenias and fuchsias overflow their pots, and behind there are blue and mauve hydrangeas which you almost feel you can reach out and pick. The standard rose and the tall pencil pine add a dramatic touch. Bees buzz around in the summer haze to complete the scene.

Fold your piece of linen up one third from the lower edge. My garden is 27 cm (10¾″) wide (just over the width of this book); centre this measurement on the creaseline and mark with a pencil. This will ensure you have ample fabric around your finished embroidery for framing. Work a running stitch along this line with one strand of a pale green embroidery thread. This will be a more definite and lasting guide and can be stitched over and left in your work.

Begin your Summer Garden by working the sundial in the centre. Work the flowers around the sundial — rose campion, shasta daisies and lamb's-ear with the smaller flowers, the chamomile and Chinese forget-me-nots, in front. Beside the lamb's ear, embroider the agapanthus and the sunflowers with penstemon, achillea and petunias in front, finishing off the end with another stem of lamb's ear and a few heartsease.

Pencil in and embroider the standard rose ('Peter Frankenfeld') behind the shasta daisies. Add some bees to complete the right-hand side of your picture.

Mark in the terracotta pot and the Versailles planter and embroider them; then add the fuchsia and the gardenia. Stitch the evening primrose next, with the catmint, heartsease and convolvulus in the foreground. Work the hydrangea behind and between the gardenia and the evening primrose. Add the pencil pine to give height to your garden and, finally, work the Chinese forget-me-nots and chamomile next to the fuchsia at the end of your garden.

Complete your garden by embroidering a title, if you wish, such as 'Summer', in stem stitch, using one strand of embroidery thread. Sign and date your work.

FLOWERS AND FEATURES IN THE SUMMER GARDEN

achillea	hydrangea	sundial
agapanthus	lamb's ear	terracotta pot
catmint	pencil pine	Versailles planter
chamomile	penstemon	
Chinese forget-me-not	petunia	
convolvulus	rose campion	
evening primrose	rose 'Peter Frankenfeld'	
fuchsia	shasta daisy	
gardenia	sunflower	
heartsease	bee	

PREREQUISITES FOR SUMMER GARDEN

THREADS

blanc neige/white

ecru

209	lavender — dark
210	lavender — medium
211	lavender — light
309	rose — deep
315	antique mauve — very dark
319	pistachio green — very dark
320	pistachio green — medium
327	violet — very dark
333	blue violet — very dark
340	blue violet — medium
341	blue violet — light
356	terracotta — medium
368	pistachio green — light
415	pearl grey
433	brown — medium
444	lemon — dark
445	lemon — light
469	avocado green
470	avocado green — light
504	blue green — light
550	violet — very dark
602	cranberry — medium
603	cranberry
604	cranberry — light
610	drab brown — very dark
611	drab brown — dark
648	beaver grey — light

718	plum
727	topaz — very light
762	pearl grey — very light
783	topaz — medium
793	cornflower blue — medium
842	beige brown — very light
972	canary — deep
973	canary — bright
988	forest green — medium
3051	green grey — dark
3052	green grey — medium
3346	hunter green
3347	yellow green — medium
3348	yellow green — light
3350	dusty rose — ultra dark
3362	pine green — dark
3363	pine green — medium
3371	black brown
3607	plum — light
3746	blue violet — dark

FABRIC
45 cm x 27 cm (18″ x 10¾″) embroidery linen

NEEDLES
Embroidery crewel Nos 7, 8 and 9
Straw or millinery Nos 8 and 9

Small embroidery hoop 10 cm (4″)

Soft pencil and small embroidery scissors

CHAPTER 4

THE SUMMER GARLAND

Very early one summer morning I was inspired to go into my garden and gather an armful of brightly coloured flowers. I arranged them as a garland and, delighted with this cheerful array, I decided to photograph and embroider them as a summer project.

The size of your garland is for you to decide and will depend on how much time you wish to spend embroidering. My garland measures 16 cm (6½′) in diameter.

Lightly mark your fabric with two circles using a compass or two plates and divide them into thirds or fifths. Run a stitch with one strand of pale green embroidery thread around the two circles. This will form a more definite and lasting guide and can be stitched over and left in your work.

I have worked the flowers in my garland closely together but it would look equally lovely with a little more space between them. Other flowers from this book could be included in your summer garland, such as passionflower, gardenia and fuchsia.

Begin by working the larger flowers first in each section — hydrangeas, sunflowers, roses and evening primroses. Fill in with the smaller flowers. Ensure that you have created an even balance of colour, size and texture of flowers.

Take care to control the tension while working: a hoop will make this easier.

If you wish, entitle your work 'Summer Flowers' by embroidering the words in stem stitch, with one strand of embroidery thread. Lastly, sign and date your work.

FLOWERS IN THE SUMMER GARLAND

achillea

agapanthus

catmint

chamomile

Chinese foreget-me-not

convolvulus

evening primrose

French lavender

hydrangea

lamb's ear

penstemon

rose campion

rose 'Peter Frankenfeld'

rose 'Rosamunde'

shasta daisy

sunflower

PREREQUISITES FOR THE SUMMER GARLAND

THREADS

blanc neige/white

ecru

208	lavender — very dark
209	lavender — dark
210	lavender — medium
211	lavender — light
315	antique mauve — very dark
320	pistachio green — medium
333	blue violet — very dark
340	blue violet — medium
341	blue violet — light
356	terracotta — medium
368	pistachio green — light
433	brown — medium
444	lemon — dark
445	lemon — light
504	blue green — light

602	cranberry — medium
603	cranberry
604	cranberry — light
648	beaver grey — light
718	plum
776	pink — medium
783	topaz — medium
793	cornflower blue — medium
819	baby pink — light
972	canary — deep
973	canary — bright
988	forest green — medium
3051	green grey — dark
3052	green grey — medium
3053	green grey
3346	hunter green
3347	yellow green — medium
3348	yellow green — light
3350	dusty rose — ultra dark
3363	pine green — medium
3607	plum — light
3708	plum — very light

FABRIC
(Size will vary with size of garland.) Approx. 30 cm (12″) square embroidery linen

NEEDLES
Embroidery crewel Nos 7, 8 and 9
Straw or millinery Nos 8 and 9

Small embroidery hoop 10 cm (4″)
Soft pencil and small embroidery scissors

CHAPTER 5

THE AUTUMN GARDEN

Fall, leaves, fall; die, flowers, away;
Lengthen night and shorten day:
Every leaf speaks bliss to me
Fluttering from the autumn tree.

Emily Brontë

Autumn is my favourite season: the ornamental grape with its russet and scarlet leaves trails over the arch, the fallen leaves below capturing the essence of Autumn. There is still so much beauty in an Autumn garden. The agapanthus flowers and roses have faded leaving the ripening and mature seed heads. The cooler air has turned the Summer hydrangea flowers to lovely soft hues of pink and green. Perennials such as chrysanthemums, daisies and dainty Japanese anemones add colour to the garden as do the delicate bulbs colchicum, Autumn crocus and nerines. A butterfly flits above the Autumn garden to complete the setting.

Fold your piece of linen up one third from the lower edge. My garden is 27 cm (10¾″) wide (just over the width of this book); centre this measurement on the crease line and mark with a pencil. This will ensure you have ample fabric around your finished embroidery for framing.

Work a running stitch along this line with one strand of a pale green embroidery thread. This will form a more definite and lasting guide and can be stitched over and left in your work.

To begin, pencil in the arch and the tub. When you have completed stitching these, add the grapevine and the kumquat tree and commence work on the ornamental grape leaves. Mark the hydrangea flowers and leaves and start to work on these to build up the bush. I recommend you use a small hoop for the flowers. Rather than stitching all the leaves on the ornamental grape or the entire hydrangea at one time, alternate working on them with some of the flowers in the foreground for variety.

Next, stitch the colchicum beside the tub and, leaving a space, add the Autumn agapanthus. Tuck chamomile in between the colchicum and the agapanthus with the chrysanthemum (daisy) behind, and behind these add some stems of Easter daisy (*Aster amellus*). To complete this side of the garden fill the tub with alyssum with a little on the ground alongside, in front of the colchicum. Stitch some cyclamen on the other side of the tub and at the end next to the agapanthus.

Between the hydrangea and the arch, work the nerines, chrysanthemum (button) and Easter daisies (*Aster sp.*). Add some Autumn crocus and cyclamen in front, with rosehips, Japanese anemone and French lavender behind. To finish your picture, embroider colchicum and chamomile at the end next to the hydrangea and add the butterfly.

Complete your garden by embroidering a title, if you wish, such as 'Autumn', in stem stitch, with one strand of embroidery thread. Sign and date your work.

FLOWERS AND FEATURES IN THE AUTUMN GARDEN

agapanthus	chrysanthemum (button)	Easter daisy (*Aster amellus*)	Japanese anemone	rosehips
alyssum	chrysanthemum (daisy)	Easter daisy (*Aster sp.*)	kumquat	butterfly
Autumn crocus	colchicum	French lavender	nerine	arch
chamomile	cyclamen	hydrangea	ornamental grape	tub

PREREQUISITES FOR AUTUMN GARDEN

THREADS

ecru

208	lavender — very dark
210	lavender — dark
211	lavender — light
221	shell pink — dark
223	shell pink — medium
307	lemon
319	pistachio green — very dark
347	salmon — dark
349	coral — dark
356	terracotta — medium
444	lemon — dark
470	avocado green — light
472	avocado green — ultra light
501	blue green — dark
503	blue green — medium
552	violet — medium
553	violet
554	violet — light
603	cranberry
604	cranberry — light
611	drab brown — dark
612	drab brown — medium
640	beige grey — very dark
725	topaz
726	topaz — light
727	topaz — very light
731	olive green — dark
741	tangerine — medium

742	tangerine — light
758	terracotta — light
772	pine green — light
783	Christmas gold
839	beige brown — dark
840	beige brown — medium
937	avocado green — medium
973	lemon — dark
3013	khaki green — light
3051	green grey — dark
3053	green grey
3346	hunter green
3347	yellow green — medium
3348	yellow green — light
3362	pine green — dark
3363	pine green — medium
3609	plum — ultra light
3689	mauve — light

FABRIC
45 cm x 27 cm (18″ x 10¾″) embroidery linen

NEEDLES
Embroidery crewel Nos 7, 8 and 9
Straw or millinery No 8

Small embroidery hoop 10 cm (4″)

Soft pencil and small embroidery scissors

CHAPTER 6

THE WINTER GARDEN

*Brother, Joy to you
I've brought some snowdrops; only just a few,
But quite enough to prove the world awake,
Cheerful and hopeful in the frosty dew
And for the pale sun's sake.*

Christina Rossetti

Surprisingly, the Winter garden reveals an abundance of colour. The crimson foliage of the nandina and the berries of the cotoneaster illustrate this. The herbaceous border is alive with early bulbs and perennials: jonquils, snowflakes, iris, primulas, polyanthus, violets, bergenia and wallflowers. The background is dominated by a bare silver birch, an elegant garrya with its tassles and a showy wattle, heavily laden with golden blossoms. The heady fragrance of the Daphne, jonquils and violets pierce the cool, crisp air and give promise of warmer days ahead.

Fold your piece of linen up one third from the lower edge. My garden is 27 cm (10¾″) wide (just over the width of this book); centre this measurement on the crease line and mark with a pencil. This will ensure you have ample fabric around your finished embroidery for framing. Work a running stitch along this line with one strand of a pale green embroidery thread. This will form a more definite and lasting guide and can be stitched over and left in your work.

On completing my Winter Garden, I was not entirely happy with the balance of the composition. I wished I could move the Daphne over a little towards the centre and swap the positions of the jonquils so the yellow ones were not so close to the wattle. You can make these changes and, of course, any others you wish. Consider how much more striking three overlapping silver birches would be than just one.

To begin, pencil in and work the silver birch tree in the centre of your picture. Mark the wattle tree and embroider the trunk and major branches and minor branches and foliage. Start work on the blossom. As there are myriad French knots on the wattle tree, work a small branch at a time, alternating work on other flowers, to make it more interesting for yourself.

Embroider the bulbs next — Winter iris, jonquils and snowflakes. Pencil in the branches of the Daphne and the outline of the garrya; work these shrubs. Fill in the spaces between the bulbs with Winter roses, primula, wallflower, bergenia and polyanthus. The nandina, diosma and cotoneaster are added behind this border of bulbs and perennials, with the violets in the foreground and at the end of your garden.

Complete your garden by embroidering a title, if you wish, such as 'Winter' in stem stitch, with one strand of embroidery thread. Sign and date your work.

FLOWERS AND FEATURES IN THE WINTER GARDEN

bergenia	nandina	wallflower
cotoneaster horizontalis	polyanthus (blue)	wattle
Daphne	polyanthus (yellow)	Winter iris
diosma	primula	Winter rose (pink)
garrya	silver birch	Winter rose (white)
jonquil (cream)	snowflake	
jonquil (yellow)	violet	

PREREQUISITES FOR WINTER GARDEN

THREADS
blanc neige/white
209	lavender — dark
223	shell pink — light
307	lemon
316	antique mauve — medium
327	violet — very dark
340	blue violet — medium
347	salmon — very dark
445	lemon — light
469	avocado green
470	avocado green — light
471	avocado green — very light
472	avocado green — ultra light
524	fern green — very light
553	violet
605	cranberry — very light
611	drab brown — dark
613	drab brown — light
741	tangerine — medium
743	yellow — medium
746	off white
762	pearl grey — very light
778	antique mauve — very light
840	beige brown — medium
937	avocado green — medium
987	forest green — dark
3013	khaki green — light
3051	green grey — dark
3052	green grey — medium

3064   sportsman flesh — very dark
3328   salmon — dark
3346   hunter green
3347   yellow green — medium
3363   pine geen — medium
3609   plum — ultra light
3721   shell pink — dark
3740   antique violet — dark
3787   brown grey — dark

FABRIC
45 cm x 27 cm (18″ x 10¾″) embroidery linen

NEEDLES
Embroidery crewel Nos 7, 8 and 9
Straw or millinery No 8

Small embroidery hoop 10 cm (4″)

Soft pencil and small embroidery scissors

CHAPTER 7

FINISHING TOUCHES

When you have finished placing all the plants and features, appraise your composition carefully for balance of colour, intensity and form. You will probably find you wish to add an extra flower or a few leaves here and there. Be sure at this stage to add your name or initials and the year. This is important because you have created a unique piece of fine art which will be valued by generations to come.

When you are completely happy with the balance of your work, it's time for the final touches!

- Tidy up the threads at the back, trimming back so there are no long tags.

- Carefully handwash your finished work in warm water with soft soap. (Do not soak as some threads may bleed.) Any stubborn pencil marks can be removed with a toothbrush.

- Rinse in distilled water. This will ensure that your heirloom embroidery will not discolour over the years. (Distilled water does not contain the acids and minerals found in tap water that cause brown stains in future years.) Do not wring out the embroidery because the creases can be very difficult to remove.

- It is best to iron your embroidery as soon as it is washed. Place a towel on the ironing board and overlay with a faded linen tea towel (so the dye will not run). Place the wet embroidery face down on the towels. You can either place another tea towel over the embroidery, or iron it direct, but *please* take care not to scorch it. While ironing, make sure you press any thread tags back over the embroidered part so that they don't show through the linen when the work is framed.

Now for the exciting bit! When you turn the embroidery over you will be thrilled to see your garden come to life. The pressure applied to the towels will have made the flowers stand out without showing indentations. Examine your work in daylight to ensure the finished piece is to your satisfaction in every detail.

After you have finished ironing your embroidery keep it flat in a folder until you take it to the framer. Arrange framing as soon as possible after washing and ironing.

The final decision you will need to make will concern the type and colour of the mount and frame. Choose a mount that complements your embroidered garden. In my season embroideries, I have chosen colours which reflect the feeling of the particular season: dull red for Winter, camel for Autumn and deep green for Summer. A good framer will help you make your choice. It is important to conserve your finished piece of needlework so, for further advice on lacing and framing, *please* read Appendix A.

If you are planning to do more than one season, make sure the frame you choose for the first garden will be available for the later ones.

CHAPTER 8

FLOWER GLOSSARY

This glossary gives the colour thread numbers and the method of working the individual flowers, trees, shrubs, vines, garden ornaments and insects in this book. Also included are the needle type and the size you will need to use for each step.

Before commencing work, carefully read the details for each flower, relating the text to the drawing and the embroidered illustration. Remember that the embroidered garden samplers and drawn illustrations for each flower are actual size which will help you create the correct sense of scale.

I have used DMC stranded cotton exclusively for the designs in this book. The threads have been carefully matched with the flowers and foliage for a realistic look. Many of the flowers come in other colours so you may like to experiment and match them to your own choice of threads. Some colours and subtle effects have been achieved by blending threads in the needle. It is a good trick to thread up several needles before you start working.

Many flowers, such as forget-me-nots, have five petals. To space these petals evenly, imagine a 'stick figure' with a head and spread arms and legs; these positions will help with placement.

All French knots in this glossary are worked with only one twist unless otherwise stated, as in the case of kumquats and pencil pine nuts.

Please take care not to carry threads across the back of your work.

SUMMER GARDEN

Summer Flowers

SUMMER GARLAND

AUTUMN GARDEN

WINTER GARDEN

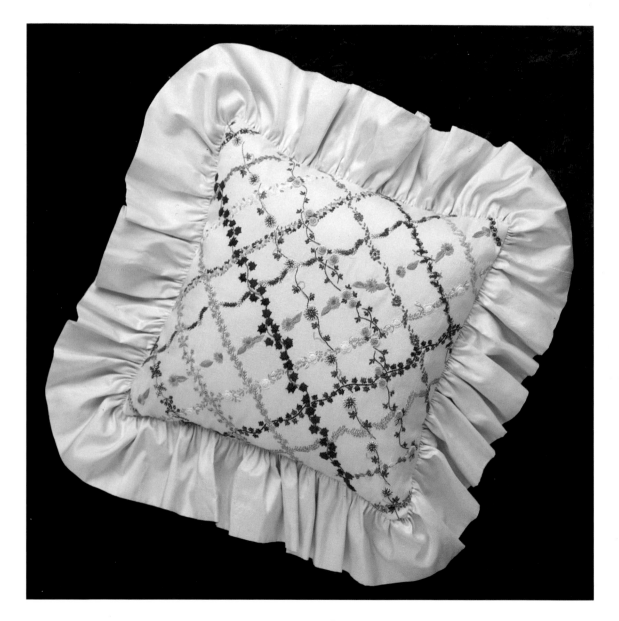

EMBROIDERED CUSHION

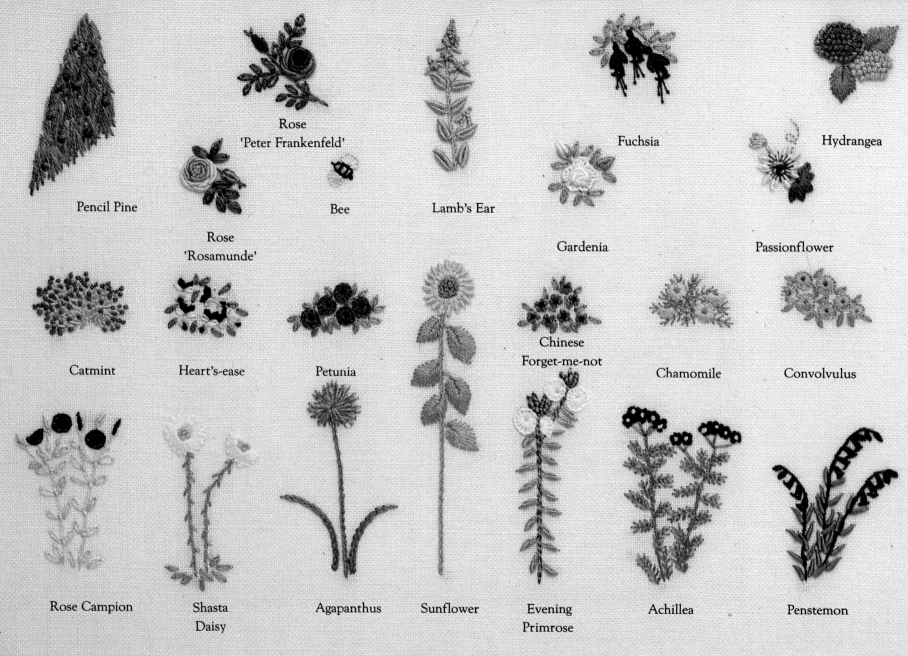

Pencil Pine

Rose 'Peter Frankenfeld'

Rose 'Rosamunde'

Bee

Lamb's Ear

Fuchsia

Gardenia

Hydrangea

Passionflower

Catmint

Heart's-ease

Petunia

Chinese Forget-me-not

Chamomile

Convolvulus

Rose Campion

Shasta Daisy

Agapanthus

Sunflower

Evening Primrose

Achillea

Penstemon

SUMMER FLOWER SAMPLER

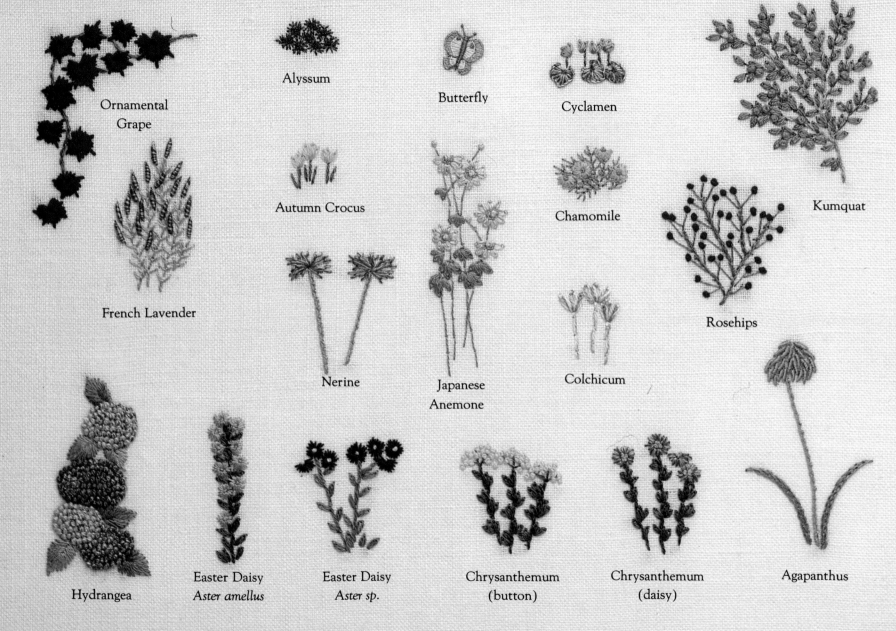

Ornamental
Grape

Alyssum

Butterfly

Cyclamen

Kumquat

French Lavender

Autumn Crocus

Chamomile

Rosehips

Nerine

Japanese
Anemone

Colchicum

Hydrangea

Easter Daisy
Aster amellus

Easter Daisy
Aster sp.

Chrysanthemum
(button)

Chrysanthemum
(daisy)

Agapanthus

AUTUMN FLOWER SAMPLER

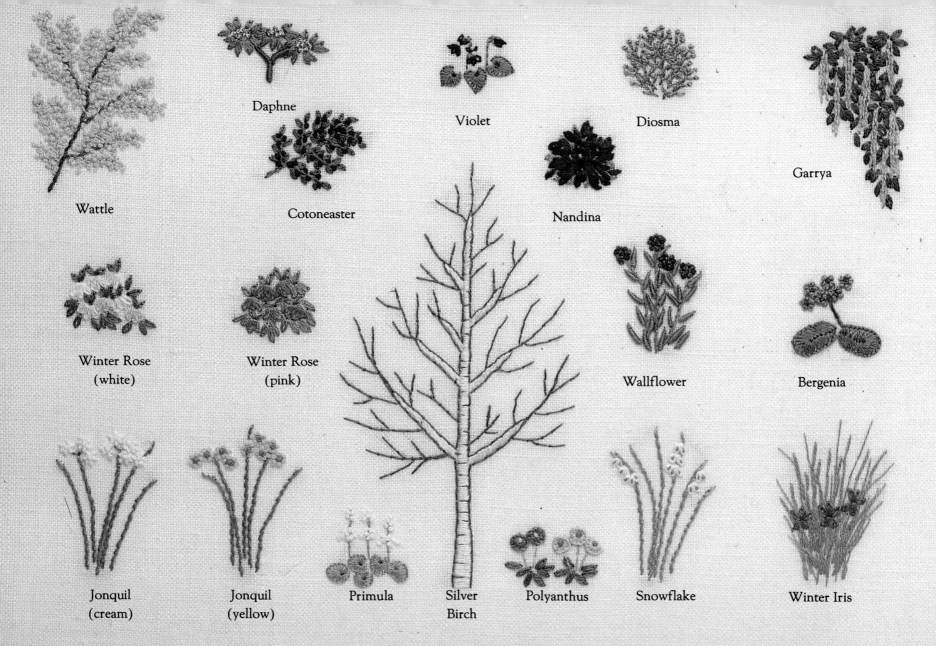

Daphne

Violet

Diosma

Wattle

Cotoneaster

Garrya

Nandina

Winter Rose
(white)

Winter Rose
(pink)

Wallflower

Bergenia

Jonquil
(cream)

Jonquil
(yellow)

Primula

Silver
Birch

Polyanthus

Snowflake

Winter Iris

WINTER FLOWER SAMPLER

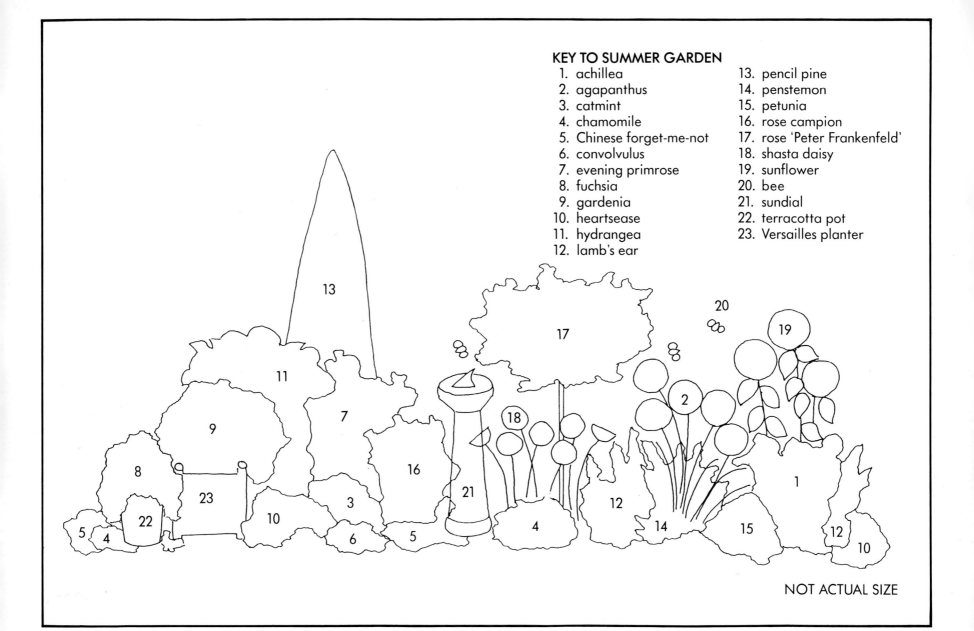

KEY TO SUMMER GARDEN
1. achillea
2. agapanthus
3. catmint
4. chamomile
5. Chinese forget-me-not
6. convolvulus
7. evening primrose
8. fuchsia
9. gardenia
10. heartsease
11. hydrangea
12. lamb's ear
13. pencil pine
14. penstemon
15. petunia
16. rose campion
17. rose 'Peter Frankenfeld'
18. shasta daisy
19. sunflower
20. bee
21. sundial
22. terracotta pot
23. Versailles planter

NOT ACTUAL SIZE

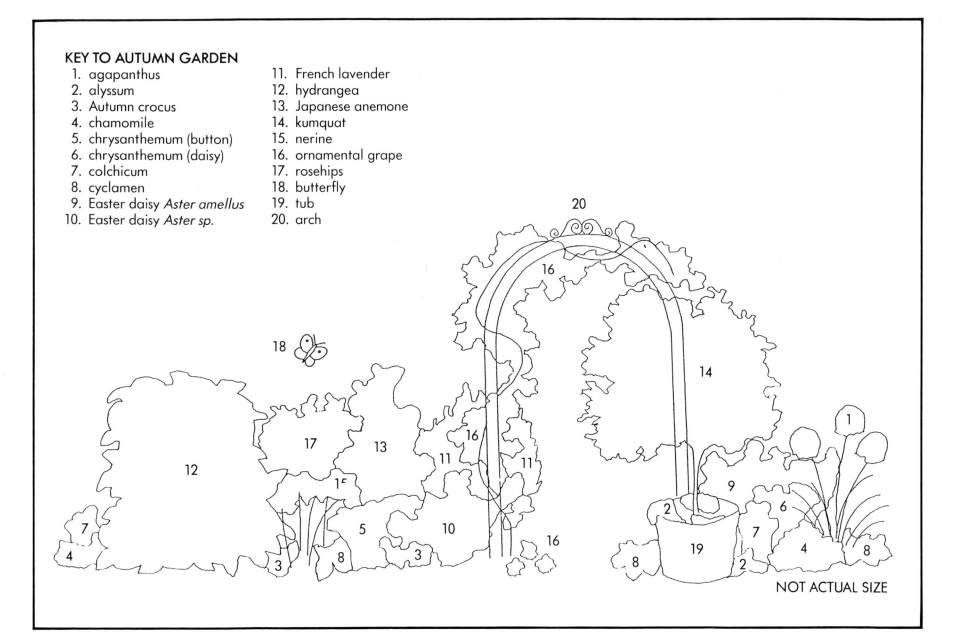

KEY TO AUTUMN GARDEN

1. agapanthus
2. alyssum
3. Autumn crocus
4. chamomile
5. chrysanthemum (button)
6. chrysanthemum (daisy)
7. colchicum
8. cyclamen
9. Easter daisy *Aster amellus*
10. Easter daisy *Aster sp.*
11. French lavender
12. hydrangea
13. Japanese anemone
14. kumquat
15. nerine
16. ornamental grape
17. rosehips
18. butterfly
19. tub
20. arch

NOT ACTUAL SIZE

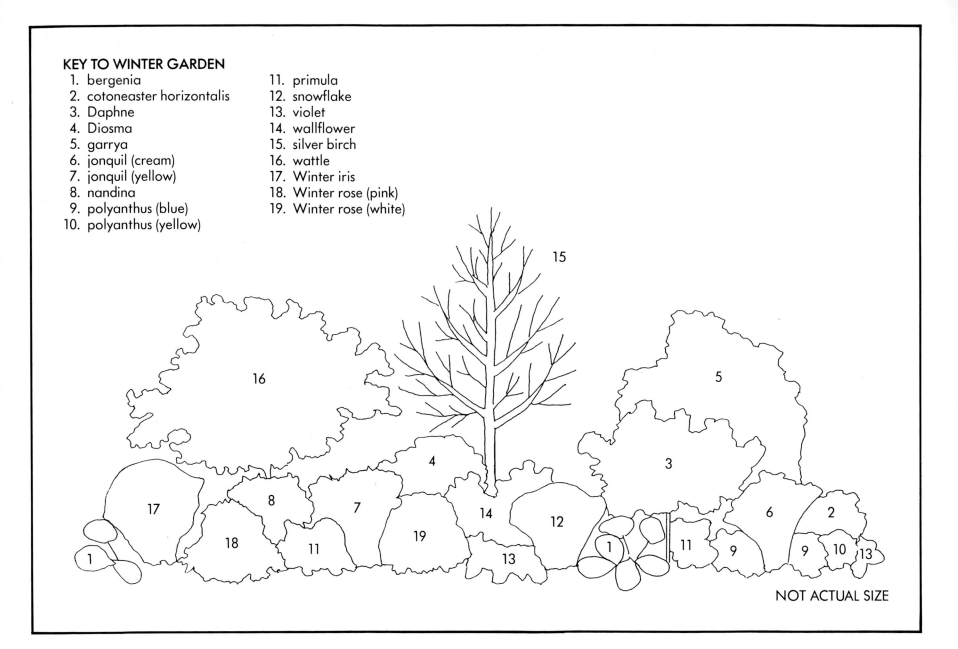

KEY TO WINTER GARDEN

1. bergenia
2. cotoneaster horizontalis
3. Daphne
4. Diosma
5. garrya
6. jonquil (cream)
7. jonquil (yellow)
8. nandina
9. polyanthus (blue)
10. polyanthus (yellow)
11. primula
12. snowflake
13. violet
14. wallflower
15. silver birch
16. wattle
17. Winter iris
18. Winter rose (pink)
19. Winter rose (white)

NOT ACTUAL SIZE

This could affect the tension. A thread of a deep, intense colour may show through when your finished piece is framed.

Make sure you give yourself a break from stitching every half an hour or so, to rest your eyes and your neck and shoulder muscles. Focus your eyes on something in the distance for a few moments to relax the eye muscles. Have a stretch and walk around before returning to work.

NOTES FOR LEFT-HANDED EMBROIDERERS

There is no reason why you should have any difficulty with embroidery because you are left-handed. The illustrations in the Stitch Glossary have been reproduced for you in mirror-image.

The following suggestions may prove helpful:

- When working buttonhole stitch, you will find it easier to work from right to left (as in fuchsia trumpets, penstemon flowers and the lower petal of the heartsease).

- Work in a clockwise direction for flowers formed with buttonhole circles (petunia and evening primrose). Violet leaves, bergenia leaves and gardenia are also worked in a clockwise direction.

- Flowers with petals around the centre should be worked anti-clockwise (lazy daisy stitch for shasta daisies and Japanese anemone; lazy daisy bullion stitch for sunflower and passionflower; fly stitch for agapanthus and nerines).

- Ornamental grape leaves should be worked clockwise.

ACHILLEA 'CERISE QUEEN' *Achillea millefolium*

THREADS

ecru
602   cranberry — medium
3607   plum — light
3052   green grey — medium
3346   hunter green

STRANDS, STITCHES AND NEEDLES

stems		1 strand each 3052 and 3346 blended, couching, crewel 8
flowers	centres	2 strands ecru, French knots, crewel 8
	petals	1 strand each 602 and 3607 blended, French knots, crewel 8
leaves		1 strand each 3052 and 3346 blended, fly stitch, crewel 8

Work several stems in couching, branching at the top into three or four flower stalks. Stitch three or four French knots with ecru above the stalks for the centres of the flowers. Leave space for the petals. Work five French knots for the petals around each centre, forming a cluster of flowers. Work the leaves, starting at the tip and working back to the stem with small fly stitches.

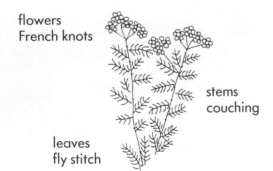

flowers
French knots

stems
couching

leaves
fly stitch

AGAPANTHUS *Agapanthus orientalis*

THREADS
340   blue violet — medium
341   blue violet — light
3346   hunter green

STRANDS, STITCHES AND NEEDLES

flowers   1 strand each 340 and 341 blended, fly stitch,
                           crewel 8
stems   2 strands 3346, whipped stem stitch, crewel 8
leaves   2 strands 3346, stem stitch, crewel 8

Lightly mark the stems and arched leaves. Draw a circle at the top of each stem, leaving a small segment where the flower joins the stem. The flowers are worked in fly stitch with a small 'V' on the outside of the circle and the long tail going into the same hole in the centre. Work in a clockwise direction and stagger the length of the stitches. Add a few straight stitches in one strand of green radiating from the centre to depict the flowers' stalks.

   The stems are worked in a single row of whipped stem stitch and the arched leaves in two rows of stem stitch, tapering to a point for the leaf's tip. Cross some leaves over the stems and over the other leaves to give a realistic effect. A bud can be added in satin stitch, if desired.

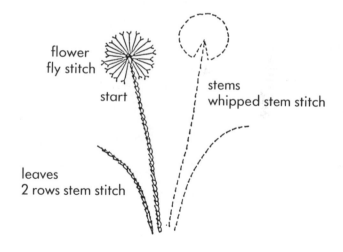

flower
fly stitch

start

stems
whipped stem stitch

leaves
2 rows stem stitch

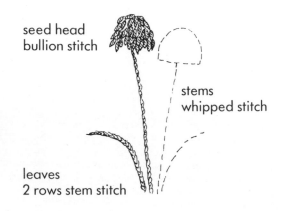

seed head
bullion stitch

stems
whipped stitch

leaves
2 rows stem stitch

leaves
straight stitch

flowers
French knots

AGAPANTHUS *Agapanthus orientalis* Autumn

THREADS
3347   yellow green — medium
3346   hunter green

STRANDS, STITCHES AND NEEDLES
seed heads   2 strands 3347, bullion stitch, straw 8
stems   2 strands 3347, whipped stem stitch, crewel 8
leaves   2 strands 3346, stem stitch, crewel 8

Mark stems, arched leaves and seed heads. The seed heads are worked first with bullion stitch (five wraps); start at the top and fill the marked area. The stems are worked with a single row of whipped stem stitch and the leaves with two rows of stem stitch, tapering to a point for the leaf's tip. Cross some leaves over the stems and over the other leaves to give a realistic effect.

ALYSSUM (SWEET ALICE) *Lobularia maritima*

THREADS
553   violet
3051   green grey — dark

STRANDS, STITCHES AND NEEDLES
flowers   1 strand 553, French knots, crewel 9
leaves   1 strand 3051, straight stitch, crewel 9

Flowers are worked in clusters of six to eight French knots. Add small, straight stitches around the edge of the flowers for the leaves. Alyssum is useful for filling in spaces between other flowers.

AUTUMN CROCUS *Sternbergia lutea*

THREADS
973   canary — bright
3346   hunter green

STRANDS, STITCHES AND NEEDLES
flowers   2 strands 973, lazy daisy stitch, crewel 8
stems and leaves   2 strands 3346, straight stitch, crewel 8

The crocus flowers are very small; work them first with three lazy daisy stitches, slightly overlapping and pointing upwards. The stems and leaves are added below the flowers with straight stitches.

flowers
lazy daisy stitch

stems & leaves
straight stitch

BERGENIA *Bergenia cordifolia*

THREADS
3609   plum — ultra light
3064   sportsman flesh — very dark
3328   salmon — dark
3346   hunter green

STRANDS, STITCHES AND NEEDLES

leaves		2 strands 3346, buttonhole stitch, crewel 8
stems		1 strand each 3064 and 3328 blended, stem stitch, crewel 8
flowers	centres	1 strand each 3064 and 3328 blended, French knots, crewel 8
	petals	3 strands 3609, French knots, crewel 8

Draw three or four paddle-shaped leaves with a central vein. Work the leaves in buttonhole stitch starting at the base and working around the leaf and, at the same time, to a point two-thirds of the way along the central vein. Work two or three stems in stem stitch, working upwards from the leaves. With the same thread, above each stem, stitch five or six French knots approximately 3 mm (⅛″) apart for the centres of the flowers. Work five French knots for the petals around each centre, forming a cluster of flowers.

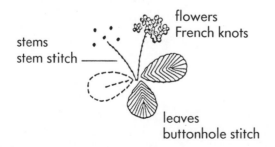

stems
stem stitch

flowers
French knots

leaves
buttonhole stitch

CATMINT *Nepeta cataria*

THREADS
209   lavender — dark
368   pistachio green — light

STRANDS, STITCHES AND NEEDLES
foliage   2 strands 368, fly stitch, crewel 8
flowers   2 strands 209, French knots, crewel 8

Work the foliage with fly stitch, starting at the top of the stems and working back to the base. Overlap some stems until a well-shaped, small bush is formed. The flowers are added with French knots on the top of the stems and on either side to halfway down the stems.

flowers
French knots

foliage
fly stitch

CHAMOMILE *Anthemis tinctoria*

THREADS
444   lemon — dark
783   topaz — medium
3363   pine green — medium

STRANDS, STITCHES AND NEEDLES
foliage   1 strand 3363, fly stitch, crewel 9
flowers   petals   1 strand 444, lazy daisy stitch, crewel 9
           centres   2 strands 783, French knot, crewel 8

Work the foliage with fly stitch, starting at the top of the stems and working back to the base. Overlap some stems until a well-shaped, small bush is formed. Work small daisies at the top of the stems and scatter more over the foliage. These are worked with eight to ten lazy daisy stitches for the petals, leaving a space for the centre. Work some half flowers to depict a side-on view. Add the flower centres with a French knot.

flowers
lazy daisy stitch
centre French knots

foliage
fly stitch

leaves
lazy daisy stitch

flowers
French knots

CHINESE FORGET-ME-NOT *Cynoglossum amabile*

THREADS

793   cornflower blue — medium
333   blue violet — very dark
3052 green grey — medium

STRANDS, STITCHES AND NEEDLES

flowers	centre	2 strands 333, French knots, crewel 8
	petals	2 strands 793, French knots, crewel 8
leaves		2 strands 3052, lazy daisy stitch, crewel 8

Work centres first with one French knot and surround very closely with five French knots for the petals. Scatter lazy daisy stitch leaves underneath the flowers.

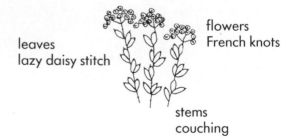

leaves
lazy daisy stitch

flowers
French knots

stems
couching

CHRYSANTHEMUM (BUTTON) *Chrysanthemum morifolium*

THREADS

307   lemon
3362 pine green — dark

STRANDS, STITCHES AND NEEDLES

stems	2 strands 3362, couching, crewel 8 with 1 strand crewel 9
leaves	2 strands 3362, lazy daisy stitch, crewel 8
flowers	3 strands 307, French knots, crewel 7

Mark required number of stems and work them in couching. Using the one strand of couching thread, work three or four small branches at the top of each stem. The leaves splay upwards from the stems and are formed by working two or three lazy daisy stitches together. Add the flowers at the top of the stems with French knots.

CHRYSANTHEMUM (DAISY) *Chrysanthemum morifolium*

THREADS

356   terracotta — medium
758   terracotta — very light
725   topaz
3362   pine green — dark

STRANDS, STITCHES AND NEEDLES

stems		2 strands 3362, couching, crewel 8 with 1 strand, crewel 9
leaves		2 strands 3362, lazy daisy stitch, crewel 8
flowers	petals	1 strand each 356 and 758 blended, straight stitch, crewel 8
	centre	2 strands 725, French knots, crewel 8

Mark required number of stems and work them in couching. The leaves splay upwards from the stems and are formed by working two or three lazy daisy stitches together. Mark the flowers at the top of the stems with a circle and with a smaller centre circle. Work the petals first with straight stitches of varying lengths. Add the centre with three French knots. A half flower adds interest.

flowers
straight stitch
centre French knots

stems
couching

leaves
lazy daisy stitch

COLCHICUM *Colchicum autumnale*

THREADS

ecru
554   violet — light
211   lavender — light
772   yellow green — very light
3013   khaki green — light

STRANDS, STITCHES AND NEEDLES

flowers   1 strand each ecru, 554 and 211 blended, lazy daisy stitch, crewel 7
stems   1 strand each ecru, 772 and 3013 blended, crewel 7, couching 1 strand 3013, crewel 9

Lightly mark the stems and work in couching. Leave enough space for the flowers; they are placed above the stems. Work the flowers with three lazy daisy stitches overlapping slightly from the top of the stem and pointing upwards.

flowers
lazy daisy stitch

stems
couching

CONVOLVULUS *Convolvulus mauretanicus*

THREADS

210   lavender — medium
320   pistachio green — medium

STRANDS, STITCHES AND NEEDLES

flowers   1 strand 210, buttonhole stitch, crewel 9
leaves   2 strands 320, lazy daisy stitch, crewel 8

Work the flowers with very small circles of buttonhole stitch. Add lazy daisy leaves underneath and between the flowers.

flowers
buttonhole stitch

leaves
lazy daisy stitch

COTONEASTER *horizontalis*

THREADS
347   salmon — very dark
937   avocado green — medium
840   beige brown — medium

STRANDS, STITCHES AND NEEDLES
branches   2 strands 840, stem stitch, crewel 8
leaves   2 strands 939, lazy daisy stitch, crewel 8
berries   2 strands 347, French knots, crewel 8

Work the branches in stem stitch. Add the leaves with tiny lazy daisy stitches alternating down the branches, then add the berries with French knots between the leaves.

berries
French knots

branches
stem stitch

leaves
lazy daisy stitch

CYCLAMEN *Cyclamen hederifolium*

THREADS
3609   plum — ultra light
501   blue green — dark
503   blue green — medium

STRANDS, STITCHES AND NEEDLES
leaves   1 strand each 501 and 503 blended, buttonhole
                    stitch, crewel 8
flowers   2 strands 3609, lazy daisy stitch, crewel 8
stems   1 strand 501, stem stich, crewel 9

First work clusters of heart-shaped leaves in buttonhole stitch. Work flowers above the leaves using two or three lazy daisy stitches overlapping them slightly from the same point and pointing them upwards or fanning to the side. Work stems in stem stitch offset slightly from the centre of the flower. Check illustration for position.

flowers
lazy daisy stitch

stems
stem stitch

leaves
buttonhole stitch

DAPHNE *Daphne odora*

THREADS
blanc neige
316   antique mauve — medium
611   drab brown — dark
987   forest green — dark

STRANDS, STITCHES AND NEEDLES

flowers	1 strand each blanc neige and 316 blended, French knots, crewel 8
leaves	2 strands 987, lazy daisy stitch, crewel 8
branches	2 strands 611, long bullion stitch, straw 8

Mark trunk and branches of the Daphne. Some flowers are worked before placement of branches and others after, so a few of the leaves can overlap the branches to create a more realistic-looking shrub. Work flowers in clusters of seven to ten French knots, surrounded by approximately seven to ten lazy daisy leaves. The number of wraps for the bullion stitch branches will vary depending on the length required. Work on the basis that an average of ten wraps measures approximately 6 mm (¼"), and 50 wraps approximately 33 mm (1¼"). The long bullion stitch branches are couched into position.

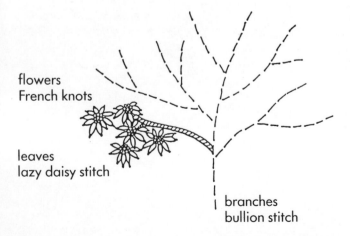

flowers
French knots

leaves
lazy daisy stitch

branches
bullion stitch

DIOSMA *Coleonema pulchrum*

THREADS
605   cranberry — very light
470   avocado green — light

STRANDS, STITCHES AND NEEDLES
foliage   2 strands 470, fly stitch, crewel 8
flowers   2 strands 605, French knots, crewel 8

Lightly mark the outline of the area for the foliage and work in fly stitch. Flowers are worked in clusters of French knots at the top of the foliage, with more scattered throughout.

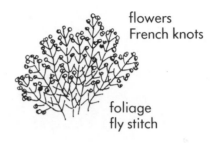

flowers
French knots

foliage
fly stitch

EASTER DAISY (MICHAELMAS) *Aster amellus*

THREADS
210   lavender — medium
444   lemon — dark
937   avocado green — medium

STRANDS, STITCHES AND NEEDLES
stems   2 strands 937, couching, crewel 8 with 1 strand, crewel 9
leaves   2 strands 937, lazy daisy stitch, crewel 8
flowers   1 strand 210, straight stitch, crewel 9
        centre   1 strand 444, French knot, crewel 9

This Easter or Michaelmas daisy grows 60 cm (2′) high. Mark required number of stems and work them in couching. Add the lazy daisy leaves, alternating them down each side of the stems. The very small daisies are placed at the top of the stem and down each side, between and over the leaves. Work the daisies in straight stitch from the outside into the same hole in the centre. Vary the length of the stitches to give a realistic look. Add the centres with a French knot.

flowers
straight stitch
centre French knot

stems
couching

leaves
lazy daisy stitch

EASTER DAISY (MICHAELMAS) *Aster sp.*

THREADS
552   violet — medium
726   topaz — light
3346   hunter green

STRANDS, STITCHES AND NEEDLES

stems	2 strands 3346, couching, crewel 8 with 1 strand, crewel 9
leaves	2 strands 3346, lazy daisy stitch, crewel 8
flowers	1 strand 552, straight stitch, crewel 9
centre	2 strands 726, French knot, crewel 8

These Easter or Michaelmas daisies are not as tall as *Aster amellus*. The flowers are larger and deeper in colour. Mark the stems and work them in couching. Add the lazy daisy leaves, alternating them down each side of the stem. The daisies are placed in clusters at the top of each stem. Work the daisies in straight stitch from the outside into the same hole in the centre. Vary the length of the stitches to give a realistic look. Add the centres with a French knot.

flowers
straight stitch
centre French knot

stems
couching

leaves
lazy daisy stitch

EVENING PRIMROSE *Oenothera laciniata nocturna*

THREADS

445   lemon — light
356   terracotta — medium
3347   yellow green — medium

STRANDS, STITCHES AND NEEDLES

buds   1 strand each 356 and 3347 blended, bullion stitch, straw 8

stems   1 strand each 356 and 3347 blended, whipped stem stitch, crewel 8

flowers   2 strands 445, buttonhole stitch, crewel 8

leaves   2 strands 3347, lazy daisy bullion stitch (4 wraps), straw 8

Mark required number of stems on your fabric and work them with whipped stem stitch. The buds are worked at the top of each stem with three or four bullion stitches (nine wraps). The flowers are placed just below the buds attached to the stem. Full flowers are formed with a circle of buttonhole stitch and side-on flowers with a part circle of buttonhole stitch. The leaves are worked with lazy daisy bullion stitch (four wraps) down either side of the stems, alternating at intervals.

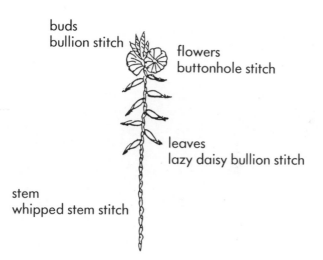

buds
bullion stitch

flowers
buttonhole stitch

leaves
lazy daisy bullion stitch

stem
whipped stem stitch

FRENCH LAVENDER *Lavandula dentata*

THREADS

208   lavender — very dark
3053   green grey

STRANDS, STITCHES AND NEEDLES

foliage	2 strands 3053, fly stitch, crewel 8
flower heads	1 strand each 208 and 3053 blended, bullion stitch, straw 8

Lightly mark the branches for the foliage. Work each branch starting at the top with a straight stitch and work down in fly stitch to the base. Overlap some branches and stitch some smaller branches for a realistic-looking lavender bush.

Work flower heads, following the angle of the stem, in bullion stitch (nine wraps) at the top of each branch. Scatter more throughout the foliage. To stitch a pointed lavender head, take the needle out a little further when anchoring the bullion stitch.

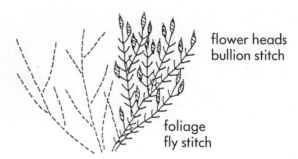

flower heads
bullion stitch

foliage
fly stitch

FUCHSIA *Fuchsia sp.*

THREADS
327 violet — very dark
309 rose — deep
315 antique mauve — very dark
470 avocado green — light

STRANDS, STITCHES AND NEEDLES

flower	trumpet	2 strands 327, buttonhole stitch, crewel 8
	petals	2 strands 309, lazy daisy bullion stitch, and lazy daisy stitch, straw 8
	stamens	1 strand 315, French knot stalk, crewel 9
	calyx	2 strands 470, French knot, 2 twists, crewel 8
stems		2 strands 470, stem stitch, crewel 8
leaves		2 strands 470, lazy daisy stitch, crewel 8

Note: Use a small hoop for good tension when working French knot stalks.

The trumpet of the fuchsia is worked first with three buttonhole stitches commencing from the left-hand side of the outside edge. Place three lazy daisy bullion stitches with one wrap, starting above the trumpet, forming the petals. Finish them over the trumpet and on either side of it. To complete the petals, work a small lazy daisy stitch pointing upward from the top of the petals. Add three stamens, coming from below the trumpet, with French knot stalks.

For the calyx, work a French knot with two twists above the flower. Stems are then worked with stem stitch where required, and leaves in lazy daisy stitch are scattered at random.

trumpet
buttonhole stitch

petals
lazy daisy bullion stitch
lazy daisy stitch

stamens
French knot stalks

leaves
lazy daisy stitch

stem
stem stitch

flowers

 outer petals
buttonhole stitch

 centre
bullion stitch

leaves
lazy daisy stitch

bud
bullion stitch
calyx — fly stitch

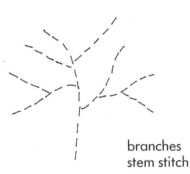 branches
stem stitch

GARDENIA 'Florida' *Gardenia augusta*

THREADS
blanc neige
3347   yellow green — medium
3346   hunter green
611   drab brown — dark

STRANDS, STITCHES AND NEEDLES

branches	2 strands 611, stem stitch, crewel 8
flowers	2 strands blanc neige, buttonhole stitch, crewel 8 and bullion stitch (5, 6 and 7 wraps), straw 8
buds	2 strands blanc neige, bullion stitch (7 wraps), straw 8
	2 strands 3347, bullion stitch (7 wraps), crewel 8
calyx	2 strands 3347, fly stitch and straight stitch, crewel 8
leaves	2 strands 3347, lazy daisy stitch, crewel 8
	2 strands 3346, lazy daisy stitch, crewel 8

Pencil in the branches and work in stem stitch. Mark the flower shapes as illustrated on the bush. Work around the outside of the flowers with buttonhole stitch, leaving the centre clear of stitches. Build up the centre of the flower in the same way as a 'grub rose' using bullion stitch. First, work two bullions with five wraps for the centre. Then, work three bullions with six wraps around, and finally two or three bullions with seven wraps until a well-formed flower is completed. The number of bullions required for the centre will depend on the size of your flower.

The buds are worked with two seven-wrap bullion stitches side by side. Add a calyx with a fly stitch around the bud and a straight stitch into the centre of the bud. The leaves are worked in lazy daisy stitch with the two greens.

GARRYA (TASSEL BUSH) *Garrya elliptica*

THREADS
613   drab brown — light
3013   khaki green — light
778   antique mauve — very light
3051   grey green — dark
936   avocado green — very dark

STRANDS, STITCHES AND NEEDLES
leaves   2 strands 3051, lazy daisy stitch, crewel 8
tassels   2 strands 936, 1 strand each 613 and 3013
                    blended, coral stitch, crewel 8
                    1 strand each 3013 and 778 blended, coral stitch,
                    crewel 8

leaves
lazy daisy stitch

tassels
coral stitch

Lightly mark the outline shape for the Garrya. Work leaves with the two shades of green in lazy daisy stitch all over the area you have outlined, but not too densely because you will add more after the tassels have been worked. The tassels are worked over the leaves with coral stitch in both of the above combinations. Each tassel is formed by working two or three lengths of coral stitch starting at the same point. Each length will have three coral stitches, but the length of each should vary slightly. Add extra leaves to fill spaces and above each tassel.

HEARTSEASE (JOHNNY JUMP-UP) *Viola tricolor*

THREADS

444   lemon — dark
211   lavender — light
727   topaz — very light
550   violet — very dark
469   avocado green

STRANDS, STITCHES AND NEEDLES

flowers	lower petals	2 strands 444, buttonhole stitch, crewel 8
	top petals	2 strands 550, lazy daisy stitch, crewel 8
	spot	2 strands 550, French knot, crewel 8
	side petals	1 strand each 727 and 211 blended, lazy daisy stitch, crewel 8
leaves		2 strands 469, lazy daisy stitch, crewel 8

These flowers are very tiny, so the stitches need to be kept as small as possible. Begin with the lower petal, using three buttonhole stitches. From the same central point, work the two top petals pointing upwards in lazy daisy stitch. Add the flower spot with a French knot on the bottom edge of the lower petal. Work the side petals at a slightly upward angle. Leaves in lazy daisy stitch are scattered at random amongst the flowers.

leaves
lazy daisy stitch

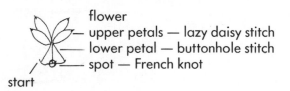

flower
— upper petals — lazy daisy stitch
— lower petal — buttonhole stitch
— spot — French knot

start

HYDRANGEA *Hydrangea macrophylla*

THREADS
340   blue violet — medium
341   blue violet — light
209   lavender — dark
211   lavender — light
3348   yellow green — light
3346   hunter green

STRANDS, STITCHES AND NEEDLES

flowers   centre   4 strands blended in different combinations of 340, 341, 209 and 211, colonial knots, crewel 7
           outside   3 strands blended in different combinations of 340, 341, 209 and 211, colonial knots, crewel 7
new flowers   1 strand each 3348, 211 and 340 blended, colonial knots, crewel 7
leaves   2 strands 3346, satin leaf stitch, crewel 8

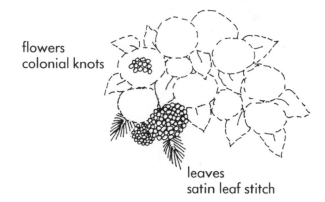

flowers
colonial knots

leaves
satin leaf stitch

Draw circular or elliptical flower shapes with leaves between to form a bush. Vary the intensity and the colour of the flowers by blending the threads.

Work the centre of the flower with four strands in colonial knots. Complete the flower shape with colonial knots in three strands. Stitch colonial knots in formation; ie, rows across or around the flower rather than higgledy-piggledy. The new flowers are smaller and worked entirely with three strands.

Work the leaves between the flowers with satin leaf stitch.

HYDRANGEA *Hydrangea macrophylla* Autumn

THREADS
223   shell pink — light
3348   yellow green — light
3346   hunter green
3347   yellow green — medium

STRANDS, STITCHES AND NEEDLES

flowers	centre	4 strands blended in different combinations of 223 and 3348, colonial knots, crewel 7
	outside	3 strands blended in different combinations of 223 and 3348, colonial knots, crewel 7
leaves		2 strands 3346, satin leaf stitch, crewel 8
		2 strands 3347, satin leaf stitch, crewel 8

Draw circular or elliptical flower shapes with leaves between to form a bush. Vary the colour of the flowers by blending the threads; some of the flowers should feature more pink and others more green. Work the centre of the flower with four strands in colonial knots. Complete the flower shape with colonial knots in three strands. Stitch colonial knots in formation; ie, rows across or around the flower rather than higgledy-piggledy.

Work the leaves between the flowers with satin leaf stitch.

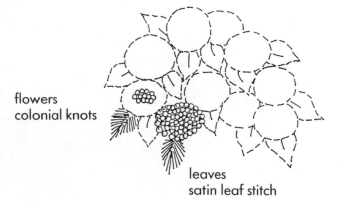

flowers
colonial knots

leaves
satin leaf stitch

JAPANESE ANEMONE (WINDFLOWER) *Anemone hupehensis*

THREADS
3689 mauve — light
472 avocado green — ultra light
742 tangerine — light
470 avocado green — light

STRANDS, STITCHES AND NEEDLES

flowers	centre	4 strands 472, French knot, crewel 7
	petals	2 strands 3689, lazy daisy stitch, crewel 8
	stamens	1 strand 742, French knots, crewel 9
stems		1 strand 470, couching, crewel 9
leaves		2 strands 470, lazy daisy and double lazy daisy stitch, crewel 8

The flowers are worked first. The centre is a French knot with four strands of 472. Stitch a few extra flower centres to depict the forming seed heads. Leave a little space around the centre for the stamens to be added after the petals. Work several lazy daisy stitch petals and add the stamens with French knots around the centre. Some half flowers add interest.

Work the stems with couching, joining the seed heads and flowers. The leaves splay from the stems and are formed by working two or three lazy daisy and double lazy daisy stitches together, pointing downwards.

seed heads
French knot

leaves
lazy daisy &
double lazy daisy stitch

stems
couching

flower
lazy daisy stitch
centre — French knots

JONQUIL (CREAM) 'Grande Monarque' *Narcissus tazetta*

THREADS
445   lemon — light
746   off white
3363   pine green — medium

STRANDS, STITCHES AND NEEDLES

stems		2 strands 3363, stem stitch, crewel 8
leaves		2 strands 3363, stem stitch, crewel 8
flowers	centre	3 strands 445, French knot, crewel 7
	petals	2 strands 746, French knot stalks, crewel 8

Mark the stems and leaves and work in stem stitch. Stitch four or five French knot centres above each stem, leaving room for the petals. Add six French knot petals around each centre to form a cluster of flowers. The petals are worked with a French knot stalk with a short tail; start a little distance from the centre and finish with the knot touching the centre.

JONQUIL (YELLOW) 'Grand Soleil d'Or' *Narcissus tazetta*

THREADS
307   lemon
741   tangerine — medium
3363   pine green — medium

STRANDS, STITCHES AND NEEDLES

stems		2 strands 3363, stem stitch, crewel 8
leaves		2 strands 3363, stem stitch, crewel 8
flowers	centre	3 strands 741, French knots, crewel 7
	petals	2 strands 307, French knots, crewel 8

Mark the stems and leaves and work in stem stitch. Stitch four or five French knot centres above each stem, leaving room for the petals. Add the six French knot petals around each centre to form a cluster of flowers.

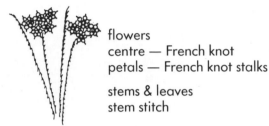

flowers
centre — French knot
petals — French knot stalks

stems & leaves
stem stitch

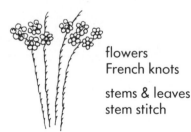

flowers
French knots

stems & leaves
stem stitch

KUMQUAT *Fortunella margarita*

THREADS
741   tangerine — medium
3346   hunter green
611   drab brown — dark
612   drab brown — medium
731   olive green — dark

STRANDS, STITCHES AND NEEDLES

tree	2 strands 611, stem stitch, crewel 8
	1 strand each 611 and 612 blended, crewel 8
	2 strands 612, stem stitch, crewel 8
twigs	1 strand 731, fly stitch and couching, crewel 9
leaves	2 strands 3346, lazy daisy stitch, crewel 8
fruit	4 strands 741, French knots (2 twists), crewel 7

Draw in the trunk and major branches of the tree and work in stem stitch in 611. Sew a second row for the trunk in stem stitch with blended 611 and 612. Add a third row for the trunk and work some branches in 612.

The twigs are added to the branches with a fly stitch with a long tail, which is couched into position. The leaves in lazy daisy stitch are worked all over the branches and twigs and the fruit is added with French knots (two twists).

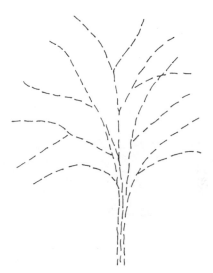

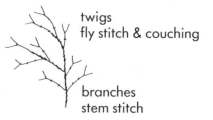

twigs
fly stitch & couching

branches
stem stitch

fruit
French knot

leaves
lazy daisy stitch

LAMB'S EAR *Stachys byzantina*

THREADS
209   lavender — dark
648   beaver grey — light

STRANDS, STITCHES AND NEEDLES

stems	2 strands 648, whipped stem stitch, crewel 8
minor stems	2 strands 648, stem stitch, crewel 8
leaves	2 strands 648, bullion stitch (9 and 11 wraps), straw 8
small leaves	2 strands 648, bullion stitch (4 wraps), straw 8
buds	2 strands 648, French knots, crewel 8
flowers	2 strands 648 and 1 strand 209 blended, French knots, crewel 8

buds & flowers
French knots

small leaves
bullion stitch

minor stems
stem stitch

leaves
bullion stitch

stem
whipped stem stitch

Study the illustration carefully and thread up with the different thread combinations before you begin. Pencil in the stems and work with whipped stem stitch. Add minor stems with stem stitch. At the tip of the plant stitch some buds with French knots and then some flowers. Add small leaves amongst and just below the flowers.

Leaves are worked down the stem in pairs and on the ground. Each leaf is formed with two bullion stitches side by side.

NANDINA (DWARF) 'Nana' *Nandina domestica*

THREADS
347   salmon — very dark
3721   shell pink — dark
3347   yellow green — medium

STRANDS, STITCHES AND NEEDLES
foliage   2 strands 3347, lazy daisy stitch, crewel 8
                  2 strands 347, lazy daisy stitch, crewel 8
                  2 strands 3721, lazy daisy stitch, crewel 8
                  1 strand each 347 and 3721 blended, lazy daisy stitch, crewel 8

Pencil in a dome shape for the outline of the bush. Cover the area with lazy daisy stitches in each of the above combinations. The stitches should point in different directions.

leaves
lazy daisy stitch

NERINE *Nerine bowdenii*

THREADS
603   cranberry
604   cranberry — light
3347   yellow green — medium

STRANDS, STITCHES AND NEEDLES

stems   2 strands 3347, whipped stem stitch, crewel 8
flower stalks   1 strand 3347, straight stitch, crewel 9
flowers   1 strand each 603 and 604 blended, fly stitch, crewel 8

Lightly mark the stems and work in whipped stem stitch. Place several flower stalks coming from the top of the stem in straight stitch. The flowers are worked in fly stitch with a small 'V' on the outside of the flower. The long tail goes into the same hole in the centre over the flower stalks. Work in a clockwise direction and stagger the length of the stitches.

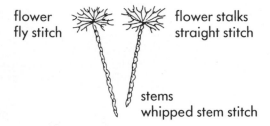

flower
fly stitch

flower stalks
straight stitch

stems
whipped stem stitch

ORNAMENTAL GRAPE *Vilis alicante* Autumn

THREADS
347   salmon — very dark
221   shell pink — very dark
640   beige grey — very dark

STRANDS, STITCHES AND NEEDLES
vine   2 strands 640, stem stitch, crewel 8
leaves   2 strands 347, straight stitch, crewel 8
                    2 strands 221, straight stitch, crewel 8
                    1 strand each 347 and 221 blended, straight stitch, crewel 8

Pencil in the vine entwined around the arch. Work in stem stitch. Add the leaves around the vine pointing in different directions. Scatter two or three on the ground. Vary the size of the leaves and stitch them in the three different thread combinations listed above. Check the illustration before working the leaves. Start at the top left-hand side of the leaf and, with straight stitches, work from the outside, with all the stitches going into the same hole in the centre. Work three short stitches, then one long stitch, all around the leaf. Finish with three short stitches.

vine
stem stitch

leaves
straight stitch

CHARLOTTE'S STORY

I designed this embroidered flower especially for my daughter Charlotte and I would like to share this delightful and romantic story with you. When she was fifteen, Charlotte was walking home from school with her first boyfriend Peter. He picked a passionflower and gave it to her. Neither of them knew what the flower was at the time but they were both fascinated with its exotic beauty.

Peter moved away to another city the following year. Charlotte received a letter much later from him and when she opened the envelope, out fell a pressed passionflower. Charlotte invited Peter to be her partner for her end of school formal party. He combed the gardens of friends to find some passionflowers, then took them to a florist and had them made into a corsage for her and a buttonhole for himself. How thrilled she was when he presented this to her. They seldom see each other these days, but remain close friends and the passionflower symbolises this friendship.

As a surprise for Charlotte I embroidered her initial with passionflowers for her 21st birthday.

flower
petals — lazy daisy bullion stitch

PASSIONFLOWER *Passiflora caerulea*

THREADS

ecru
369   pistachio green — very light
333   blue violet — very dark
726   topaz — light
3364   pine green
327   violet — very dark
3362   pine green — dark

corona — straight stitch
stamens — French knots

centre — bullion stitch

STRANDS, STITCHES AND NEEDLES

flowers	petals	1 strand each ecru and 369 blended, lazy daisy bullion stitch (4 wraps), straw 8
	corona	1 strand 333, straight stitch, crewel 9
	stamens	1 strand each 726 and 3364 blended, French knots, crewel 8
	centre	1 strand 327, bullion stitch, straw 9
leaves		2 strands 3362, double lazy daisy stitch, crewel 8
buds		2 strands 3364, lazy daisy stitch, crewel 8
tendrils		1 strand 3364, stem stitch or back stitch, crewel 9
stems		2 strands 3364, stem stitch, crewel 8

Lightly mark flowers with a small circle surrounded by a larger circle. Ten petals are worked in lazy daisy bullion stitch (4 wraps) in the outer circle. To help space the petals, work the hour and half-hour stitches first. Then space the four stitches on each side as evenly as possible.

The corona is added with violet blue straight stitches between and into each petal. Four French knots form the stamens which fill the centre with the blended yellow and green. The final touch to the centre of the flower is worked in purple with two bullion stitches to form a 'Y'. First, work a bullion with eight wraps across the centre of the flower. Then, work a second bullion with only four wraps from the middle of the first bullion to the outside of the circle, forming a 'Y'.

The buds are worked with three slightly overlapping lazy daisy stitches. Stems can be worked in stem stitch if required. The climbing tendrils are worked with stem stitch or back stitch. Finally, the palmate leaves are worked with five double lazy daisy stitches.

bud
lazy daisy stitch

tendrils
stem or back stitch

leaves
double lazy daisy stitch

PENCIL PINE *Cupressus sempervirens*

THREADS
3362   pine green — dark
3363   pine green — medium
3346   hunter green
610   drab brown — very dark
611   drab brown — dark

STRANDS, STITCHES AND NEEDLES

foliage	1 strand each 3362 and 3363 blended, straight stitch, crewel 8
	1 strand each 3362 and 3346 blended, straight stitch, crewel 8
	1 strand each 3363 and 3346 blended, straight stitch crewel 8
nuts	2 strands each 610 and 611 blended, French knot (2 twists), crewel 7

Note: Use a small hoop for good tension when working straight stitch.

Pencil in the outline of the tree. Thread up your needles in the different thread combinations. Cover the area with straight stitches of varying length in each of the above combinations. Some of the stitches should be on a slight angle. Add the nuts to complete your pencil pine.

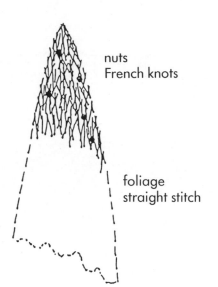

nuts
French knots

foliage
straight stitch

PENSTEMON *Penstemon davisonii*

THREADS
315 antique mauve — very dark
3350 dusty rose — ultra dark
988 forest green — medium

STRANDS, STITCHES AND NEEDLES
stems   2 strands 315, couching, crewel 8
flowers   2 strands 3350, lazy daisy stitch and buttonhole
         stitch, crewel 8
leaves   2 strands 988, bullion stitch (7 wraps), straw 8

Pencil in and work the arching stems with couching. Add the flowers with a couple of lazy daisy stitches at the tip of the stem and several bells of two buttonhole stitches down the stem. The leaves are worked at random up the stems in pairs using bullion stitches.

flowers
lazy daisy & buttonhole stitch

stems
couching

leaves
bullion stitch

PETUNIA *Petunia velutina*

THREADS
3746 blue violet — dark
3347 yellow green — medium
3052 green grey — medium

STRANDS, STITCHES AND NEEDLES
flowers   2 strands 3746, buttonhole stitch, crewel 8
leaves   1 strand each 3347 and 3052 blended, lazy daisy
         stitch, crewel 8

Work the flowers with small circles of buttonhole stitch. Add lazy daisy stitch leaves underneath and between the flowers.

flowers
buttonhole stitch

leaves
lazy daisy stitch

POLYANTHUS *Primula X polyantha*

Note: Two colours are given for this flower.

THREADS
340	blue violet — medium	
307	lemon	

or

743	yellow — medium	
741	tangerine — medium	

469	avacado green — light	
471	avacado green — very light	

STRANDS, STITCHES AND NEEDLES

flowers		2 strands 340 or 743, buttonhole stitch, crewel 8
	centres	2 strands 307 or 741, French knot, crewel 8
stems		2 strands 471, couching, crewel 8
leaves		2 strands 469, lazy daisy stitch, crewel 8

Work the flowers in small circles of buttonhole stitch with French knot centres. Add the stems with couching and the leaves below in lazy daisy stitch.

flowers
buttonhole stitch
centre — French knot

stems
couching

leaves
lazy daisy stitch

PRIMULA *Primula malacoides*

THREADS
blanc neige
3347   yellow green — medium

STRANDS, STITCHES AND NEEDLES
leaves   1 strand 3347, buttonhole stitch, crewel 9
stems   1 strand 3347, couching, crewel 9
flowers   2 strands blanc neige, French knots, crewel 8

Mark the small circular leaves and work them in buttonhole stitch. Add the stems above the leaves with couching. Work the flowers with clusters of French knots at the top of the stem and halfway down the stem.

stems   flowers
couching   French knots

leaves
buttonhole stitch

ROSE 'Rosamunde' *Rosa X*

THREADS
972   canary — deep
3708   melon — light
776   pink — medium
819   baby pink — light
3051   green grey — dark

STRANDS, STITCHES AND NEEDLES

rose	centre	2 strands 972, French knots, crewel 8
rose		2 strands 3708, bullion stitch (7 wraps), straw 8
		2 strands 776, bullion stitch (9 wraps), straw 8
		2 strands 819, bullion stitch (11 wraps), straw 8
buds		2 strands 3708, bullion stitch (7 wraps), straw 8
calyx		2 strands 3051, fly stitch, crewel 8
stems		2 strands 3051, coral stitch, crewel 8
leaves		2 strands 3051, double lazy daisy stitch, crewel 8

rose
centre — French knots
petals — bullion stitch

buds — bullion stitch
calyx — fly stitch
sepals — straight stitch

leaves
double lazy daisy stitch
leaf stems — coral stitch

Embroider the rose centre with five French knots. Then, with 3708, work three bullion stitches (7 wraps) around the centre. Next, with 776, work five bullion stitches (9 wraps) overlapping around the rose. Finally, with 819, work approximately seven bullion stitches (11 wraps) for the outer petals, again overlapping until a well-balanced rose is formed.

Add the buds with two bullion stitches placed side by side. Work a fly stitch calyx around the buds and two sepals with straight stitches on the tip of the buds.

Stems for the leaves are worked with coral stitch and the leaves are added in pairs of double lazy daisy stitch with one for the tip (five to seven leaves).

ROSE 'Peter Frankenfeld' *Rosa* X

THREADS

602	cranberry — medium
603	cranberry
604	cranberry — light
3051	green grey — dark
611	drab brown — dark

STRANDS, STITCHES AND NEEDLES

branches	2 strands 611, stem stitch, crewel 8
rose	2 strands 602, bullion stitch (7 wraps), straw 8
	2 strands 603, bullion stitch (9 wraps), straw 8
	2 strands 604, bullion stitch (11 wraps), straw 8
buds	2 strands 602, bullion stitch (7 wraps), straw 8
calyx	2 strands 3051, fly stitch, crewel 8
stems	2 strands 3051, coral stitch, crewel 8
leaves	2 strands 3051, lazy daisy stitch, crewel 8

Mark the trunk and branches of the rose bush and work the trunk with two rows of stem stitch and one row for the branches. Several full-blown roses are then worked among the branches. Start in the centre with the deepest pink 602 and work three bullion stitches (7 wraps) side by side. Then, with 603, work five bullion stitches (9 wraps) overlapping around the centre. Finally, with 604, work approximately five bullions (11 wraps) for the outer petals. Try to vary the look of each rose by arranging the bullion stitches in a different way.

Add several buds with two bullion stitches placed side by side. Join the buds to the branches with a fly stitch calyx and work two sepals with straight stitches on the tip of the buds.

Stems for the leaves are worked with coral stitch and the leaves are added in pairs of lazy daisy stitch, with one for the tip (five to seven leaves).

rose
bullion stitch

leaves
lazy daisy stitch
leaf stems — coral stitch

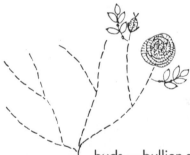

buds — bullion stitch
calyx — fly stitch
sepals — straight stitch

branches
stem stitch

ROSE CAMPION *Lychnis coronia*

THREADS
718   plum
504   blue green — light

STRANDS, STITCHES AND NEEDLES

flowers	1 strand 718, buttonhole stitch, crewel 9
buds	1 strand 718, bullion stitch (9 wraps), straw 9
	1 strand 504, bullion stitch (9 wraps), straw 9
calyx	2 strands 504, fly stitch, crewel 8
stems	2 strands 504, coral stitch, crewel 8
leaves	2 strands 504, lazy daisy stitch, crewel 8

Work small buttonhole circles for the flowers and some half circles to depict a side-on view. The stems are worked next with coral stitch. Attach them to the flowers and make some extra branches for the buds. Add a few buds in plum and a few in blue green with bullion stitch (nine wraps). Attach the buds to the stems with a fly stitch. Work the leaves in pairs with lazy daisy stitches coming from the stems.

buds
bullion stitch
calyx — fly stitch

flowers
buttonhole stitch

leaves
lazy daisy stitch

stems
couching

ROSEHIPS *Rosa sp.*

THREADS
349   coral — dark
611   drab brown — dark

STRANDS, STITCHES AND NEEDLES

branches	2 strands 611, stem stitch, crewel 8
twigs and thorns	1 strand 611, straight stitch, crewel 9
hips	3 strands 349, French knots, crewel 7

Pencil in the branches and embroider in stem stitch. Add twigs and thorns with straight stitch and the hips with French knots.

hips
French knots

branches
stem stitch

twigs & thorns
straight stitch

SHASTA DAISY *Chrysanthemum superbum*

THREADS
blanc neige
444   lemon — dark
3347   yellow green — medium

STRANDS, STITCHES AND NEEDLES

flowers	centres	2 strands 444, French knots, crewel 8
	petals	2 strands blanc neige, lazy daisy stitch, crewel 8
stems		2 strands 3347, crewel 8, couching with 1 strand, crewel 9
stem leaves		2 strands 3347, straight stitch, crewel 8
leaves		2 strands 3347, lazy daisy stitch, crewel 8

Lightly mark flowers with a small circle surrounded by a larger circle. Work the centre with five French knots. Divide outer circle into quarters like a clock face. Work one lazy daisy stitch petal for each quarter hour, and then fill in between these with more petals. This will prevent a pinwheel effect. The more petals you have, the better it will look. Mark in stems and work in couching. The stem leaves are added with small straight stitches angled downwards and alternating at intervals on each side down the stem. Work leaves with lazy daisy stitches at random around the base. A half flower adds interest.

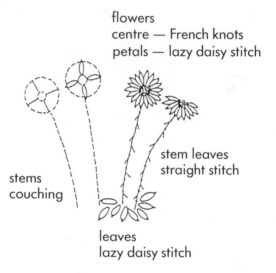

flowers
centre — French knots
petals — lazy daisy stitch

stem leaves
straight stitch

stems
couching

leaves
lazy daisy stitch

SILVER BIRCH *Betula pendula*

THREADS
blanc neige
762   pearl grey — very light
611   drab brown — dark

STRANDS, STITCHES AND NEEDLES

trunk and major branches	1 strand each blanc neige and 762 blended, satin stitch, crewel 8
outline	1 strand 611, couching, crewel 9
minor branches	1 strand 611, couching, crewel 9
striations	1 strand 611, straight stitch, crewel 9

Note: For correct tension when couching; use a hoop.

Draw the tree. Work the trunk in a horizontal satin stitch. Work the major branches with a slanting satin stitch. Outline the tree with couching and add the minor branches. Accent the striations with straight stitches of varying widths down the trunk.

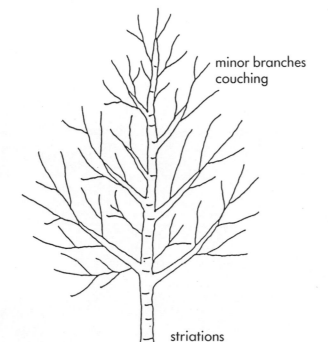

minor branches
couching

striations
straight stitch

outline
couching

trunk & major branches
satin stitch

SNOWFLAKE *Leucojum vernum*

THREADS
blanc neige
3347   yellow green — medium

STRANDS, STITCHES AND NEEDLES
stems and leaves   2 strands 3347, stem stitch, crewel 8
flowers   2 strands blanc neige, lazy daisy stitch, crewel 8
flower spots   1 strand 3347, French knots, crewel 9

Draw in stems and leaves and work in stem stitch. Leaving a little stem free at the top, work very small flowers in 'bunches' of two or three lazy daisy stitches down one side of the stem or over the stem. Place a French knot for the flower spot in each of the lazy daisy petals.

flowers
lazy daisy stitch
spots — French knots

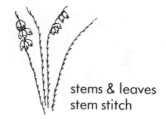

stems & leaves
stem stitch

SUNFLOWER *Helianthus annuus*

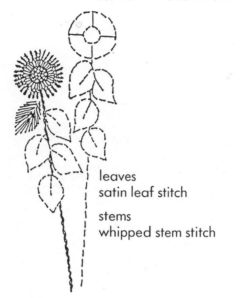

flowers
lazy daisy bullion stitch
centre — French knots

leaves
satin leaf stitch

stems
whipped stem stitch

THREADS

973	canary	— bright
783	topaz	— medium
433	brown	— medium
3347	yellow green	— medium

STRANDS, STITCHES AND NEEDLES

flowers		2 strands 973, lazy daisy bullion stitch (4 wraps), straw 8
	centres	3 strands 783, French knots, crewel 7
		3 strands 433, French knots, crewel 7
stems		3 strands and 2 strands 3347, whipped stem stitch, crewel 7 and 8
leaves		2 strands 3347, satin leaf stitch, crewel 8

Sunflowers are very tall plants and their faces are always turned towards the sun. Mark flowers in required position with a small circle surrounded by a larger circle. Divide the outer circle into quarters like a clock face. Work one lazy daisy bullion stitch (four wraps) for each quarter hour and then fill in between these with more petals. The more petals you have, the better it will look. Work the centre with French knots in either colour.

Mark the stems and work in whipped stem stitch. The sunflower in the foreground will be stitched with three strands and the others with two strands. Add the leaves with satin leaf stitch, alternating them down each side of the stem. Stitch the occasional leaf over the stem.

VIOLET (SWEET) *Viola odorata*

THREADS
327 violet — very dark
3346 hunter green
743 yellow — medium

STRANDS, STITCHES AND NEEDLES
leaves	1 strand 3346, buttonhole stitch, crewel 9
flowers	1 strand 327, lazy daisy stitch, crewel 9
bud	1 strand 327, lazy daisy stitch, crewel 9
centres	2 strands 743, French knots, crewel 8
calyx	1 strand 3346, fly stitch, crewel 9
stems	1 strand 3346, stem stitch, crewel 9

First work a cluster of heart-shaped leaves in buttonhole stitch. Add the flowers next: they consist of three lazy daisy stitch petals pointing downwards, and two lazy daisy stitch petals pointing upwards. Place a French knot in the centre. Buds have only two lazy daisy stitches pointing downwards, with a calyx of fly stitch. Work stems in stem stitch, arching them at the top where the flower is attached.

flowers
lazy daisy stitch
centre — French knot

buds
lazy daisy stitch

stems
stem stitch

leaves
buttonhole stitch

WALLFLOWER *Cheiranthus mutabilis*

THREADS
3740   antique violet — dark
553   violet
223   shell pink — light
3363   pine green — medium

STRANDS, STITCHES AND NEEDLES

centre buds	1 strand each 3740 and 3363 blended, French knots, crewel 8
flowers	1 strand each 3740 and 553 blended, French knots, crewel 8
	1 strand each 553 and 223 blended, French knots, crewel 8
	1 strand each 3740 and 223 blended, French knots, crewel 8
stems	2 strands 3363, stem stitch, crewel 8
leaves	2 strands 3363, bullion (9 wraps), straw 8

Work the centre buds first with three French knots. Thread up your needles with the three different thread combinations for the flowers and work French knots around the centre buds, forming clusters of flowers.

Work the stems in stem stitch and add the leaves in bullion stitch alternately up the stems.

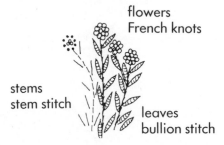

flowers
French knots

stems
stem stitch

leaves
bullion stitch

WATTLE (COOTAMUNDRA) *Acacia baileyana*

THREADS
307   lemon
3787   brown grey — dark
524   fern green — very light

STRANDS, STITCHES AND NEEDLES
tree   2 strands 3787, stem stitch, crewel 8
foliage   2 strands 524, fly stitch, crewel 8
blossom   2 strands 307, French knots, crewel 8

Draw in the trunk and branches of the tree and work in stem stitch. Add a second row of stem stitch for the trunk. The small branches and foliage are created simultaneously with fly stitch. Mark many small branches over the tree and work in fly stitch from the tips back to the main branches. Cover the whole tree heavily with French knots for the blossom; form them into small bunches with three or four French knots worked between the fly stitches.

small branches & foliage
fly stitch

blossom
French knots

trunk & branches
stem stitch

WINTER IRIS *Iris stylosa*

THREADS
340   blue violet — medium
209   lavender — dark
3347   yellow green — medium

STRANDS, STITCHES AND NEEDLES
leaves and stems   1 strand 3347, couching, crewel 9
                        2 strands 3347, couching, crewel 8
flowers   1 strand each 340 and 209 blended, lazy daisy
                        stitch, crewel 8

Using a hoop, work leaves and stems in couching. First, stitch long leaves with one strand of green. Then add more leaves with two strands until a clump is formed. Flowers are stitched over the leaves *low* in the clump. They are formed with two lazy daisy stitches pointing down from a central point and three lazy daisy stitches pointing upwards from the same point.

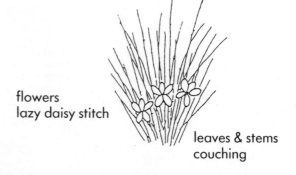

flowers
lazy daisy stitch

leaves & stems
couching

WINTER ROSE (PINK HELLEBORUS) *Helleborus orientalis*

THREADS
316   antique mauve — medium
3052   green grey — medium
3346   hunter green

STRANDS, STITCHES AND NEEDLES
flowers   2 strands 316, lazy daisy stitch, crewel 8
                               1 strand each 316 and 3052 blended, lazy daisy
                               stitch, crewel 8
leaves   1 strand each 3052 and 3346 blended, lazy daisy
                               stitch, crewel 8

Lightly mark a dome-shaped area. The pink and pink-green flowers are worked first over the marked area, leaving space for the small leaves above each flower. Work flowers with three lazy daisy stitches from the same point, fanning downwards. Work leaves in the blended greens with two small lazy daisy stitches pointing upward from the centre top of the flowers. Cluster larger lazy daisy leaves densely around the base and scatter a few leaves through the flowers, if appropriate.

flowers
lazy daisy stitch

leaves
lazy daisy stitch

WINTER ROSE (WHITE HELLEBORUS) *Helleborus niger*

THREADS
blanc neige
472   avocado green — ultra light
469   avocado green

STRANDS, STITCHES AND NEEDLES

flowers	2 strands blanc neige, lazy daisy stitch, crewel 8
	2 strands 472, lazy daisy stitch, crewel 8
	1 strand each blanc neige and 472 blended, lazy daisy stitch, crewel 8
leaves	2 strands 469, lazy daisy stitch, crewel 8

Lightly mark a dome-shaped area. The flowers in the three different combinations listed above (white, white-pale green and pale green) are worked first over the marked area, leaving space for the small leaves above each flower. Work the flowers with three lazy daisy stitches from the same point, fanning downwards. Work small leaves in the darker green with two lazy daisy stitches pointing upwards from the centre top of each flower. Cluster larger, lazy daisy leaves densely around the base and scatter a few leaves through the flowers, if appropriate.

flowers
lazy daisy stitch

leaves
lazy daisy stitch

ARCH

THREADS
319   pistachio green — very dark

STRANDS, STITCHES AND NEEDLES
arch   3 strands 319, whipped stem stitch, crewel 7
ornamentation   1 strand 319, stem stitch and straight stitch, crewel 9

Pencil in the arch and work the two rows of whipped stem stitch; take care not to stitch this too tightly. Work the decorative scroll on the top of the arch with stem stitch and the crossed bars with straight stitch; the bars can be couched where they cross.

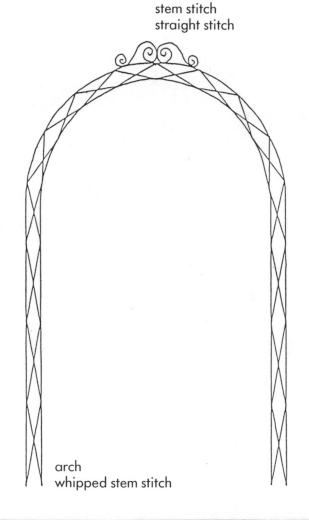

ornamentation
stem stitch
straight stitch

arch
whipped stem stitch

SUNDIAL

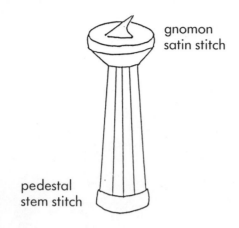

gnomon
satin stitch

pedestal
stem stitch

THREADS
842   beige brown — very light
415   pearl grey

STRANDS, STITCHES AND NEEDLES
pedestal   2 strands 842, stem stitch, crewel 8
gnomon*   2 strands 415, satin stitch, crewel 8

Draw the sundial and work the pedestal with stem stitch. Work the gnomon with satin stitch.

*the vertical, triangular plate of a sundial.

TERRACOTTA POT

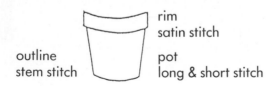

rim
satin stitch

outline
stem stitch

pot
long & short stitch

THREADS
356   terracotta — medium

STRANDS, STITCHES AND NEEDLES
pot   2 strands 356, long and short stitch, crewel 8
rim   2 strands 356, satin stitch, crewel 8
outline   1 strand 356, stem stitch, crewel 9

Note: Use a small hoop for good tension when working long and short stitch.

Pencil in your terracotta pot and work in long and short stitch; start just below the rim and work downwards. Work the rim of the pot with a vertical satin stitch. To complete, outline the pot with stem stitch.

TUB

THREADS
840   beige brown — medium
839   beige brown — dark

STRANDS, STITCHES AND NEEDLES
timber slats   2 strands 840, satin stitch, crewel 8
hoops   2 strands 839, stem stitch, crewel 8
outline   2 strands 840, stem stitch, crewel 8

Lightly mark the tub. Work the three rows of timber slats with a vertical satin stitch. Work each of the three metal hoops with four rows of stem stitch. Outline the top and sides of the tub with one row of stem stitch.

outline
stem stitch

timber slats
satin stitch

hoops
stem stitch

VERSAILLES PLANTER

THREADS
319   pistachio green — very dark

STRANDS, STITCHES AND NEEDLES
outline   2 strands 319, stem stitch, crewel 8
inside lines   2 strands 319, couching, crewel 8
knobs   2 strands 319, satin stitch, crewel 8

Lightly mark the planter and work the outline in stem stitch. Add the inside lines with couching and the knobs in satin stitch.

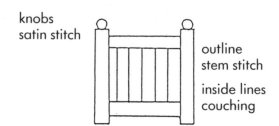

knobs
satin stitch

outline
stem stitch

inside lines
couching

BEE

body
satin stitch
outline — stem stitch

wings
buttonhole stitch

head — French knot
tail — straight stitch

THREADS
3371   black brown
972   canary — deep
762   pearl grey — very light

STRANDS, STITCHES AND NEEDLES

body	1 strand 972, satin stitch, crewel 9
	1 strand 3371, satin stitch and stem stitch, crewel 9
head	1 strand 3371, French knot (2 twists), crewel 9
wings	1 strand 762, buttonhole stitch, crewel 9

Draw the body of the bee. Work the five stripes each with three or four satin stitches. Start with the gold and alternate with the black brown. Outline the body with stem stitch and work the head with a French knot. Add a small tail with a straight stitch. Finally, embroider the wings, each with a half-circle of buttonhole stitch.

BUTTERFLY

THREADS

612	drab brown — medium	
727	topaz — very light	
840	beige brown — medium	

STRANDS, STITCHES AND NEEDLES

wings	outer	1 strand 612, buttonhole stitch, crewel 9
	inner	1 strand 727, buttonhole stitch, crewel 9
	sides	1 strand 840, straight stitch, crewel 9
spots		1 strand 840 French knot (2 twists), crewel 9
feelers		1 strand 840, French knot stalks, crewel 9
body		2 strands 840, bullion (13 wraps), straw 8

Carefully study the illustration and draw the butterfly with larger front wings and smaller back wings, each with an inner and outer part. Work the outer wings and then the inner wings with buttonhole stitch. Highlight the edges of the wings with a straight stitch and work a spot on each wing with a French knot. Add the feelers with French knot stalks. Starting at the head of the butterfly, embroider the body with a bullion stitch (13 wraps), couching in the centre.

Reference — Macoboy, S. *Stirling Macoboy's What Flower is That?* Weldon Publishing, 1989.

feelers
French knot stalks

spot
French knot

body
bullion stitch

wings
buttonhole stitch
sides — straight stitch

CHAPTER 9

STITCH GLOSSARY (right-handed)

Embroidery stitches have many different names and feature variations in structure and technique of working. This glossary describes how the stitches have been worked for the designs in this book.

For left-handed embroiderers, the instructions have been reversed and the illustrations reproduced for you in mirror image.

STEM OR OUTLINE STITCH

A simple stitch for stems, outlines and filling.

Working from left to right, take small, even straight or slightly slanting stitches along the design line. Leave a space between the point where the needle emerges and the previous stitch. Keep the thread below or on the same side of your work. For wide stem stitch, make the stitches on a greater angle.

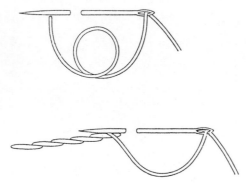

Stem or outline stitch

WHIPPED STEM STITCH

Whipped stem stitch gives a corded effect.

Work a row of stem stitch along the design line and bring the needle to the top of your work. Work in the opposite direction to that of the stem stitch. With the blunt end of the needle whip back through each stem stitch, but not into the fabric.

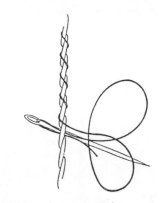

Whipped stem stitch

COUCHING

The branches and flower stems in this book worked in couching have one or two strands of thread laid down and one strand for the tying stitch of matching thread. The use of a small hoop will help with tension. Use two needles and keep them on top of your work to prevent tangling. Anchor the thread not in use and keep it out of the way. Short stems in couching can be worked with one needle and thread.

Lay the thread along the design line, holding and guiding its direction with your thumb. Tie it down with small straight stitches made at regular intervals.

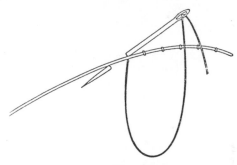

Couching

CORAL STITCH

Coral stitch is a simple knotted line stitch useful for flower stems.

Hold the thread to the left along the design line. Take a small stitch towards you with the thread over and around the needle; pull through forming a knot. Continue at regular intervals.

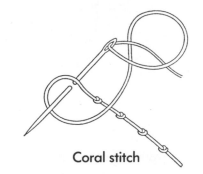

Coral stitch

FRENCH KNOTS

When working French knots you will have more control and be able to develop a rhythm if a small (10 cm/4″) hoop is used. To increase the size of knots, use more strands of thread.

Bring the thread up at the desired spot. Hold the thread firmly with your left hand. With the needle pointing toward you, place it under the thread from the left-hand side and twist it around once. Insert the needle close to where the thread first emerged, but not in the same hole. Draw the thread around the needle to firm the knot and pull through to the back. Pass on to the position for the next knot.

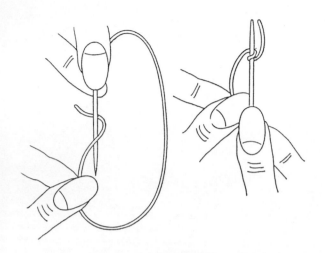

French knots

FRENCH KNOT STALKS

French knot stalks are worked in the same manner as French knots. The use of a small embroidery hoop will help you achieve good tension.

To form the stalk, after encircling the needle with the thread, insert the needle the desired distance away from where it first emerged. Pull through to the back and pass on to the position for the next stitch.

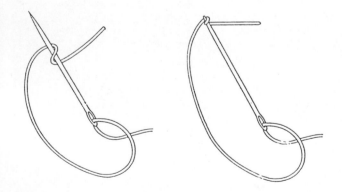

French knot stalks

COLONIAL KNOTS OR CANDLEWICKING KNOTS

This stitch differs from a French knot in that the twists are worked in a figure of eight. It stands up high on the fabric and needs to be worked very firmly. You will have more control and be able to develop a rhythm if a small (10 cm/4″) hoop is used.

Bring the thread up at the desired spot. Hold the thread firmly with your left hand. With the needle pointing away from you, place it under the thread from the left-hand side and twist it in an anti-clockwise direction away from you. The needle will now be facing you. The second part of the stitch is the same as a French knot. Now place the needle under the thread from the left-hand side and twist it around once back to the original position.

Insert the needle close to where the thread first emerged, but not in the same hole. Draw the thread around the shaft of the needle to firm the knot and pull through to the back. Pass on to the position for the next knot.

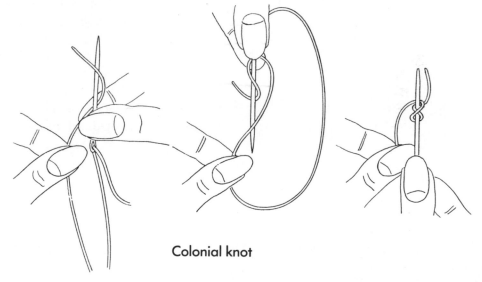

Colonial knot

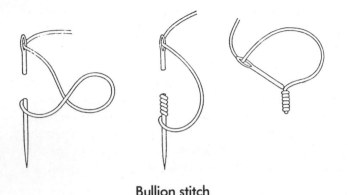

Bullion stitch

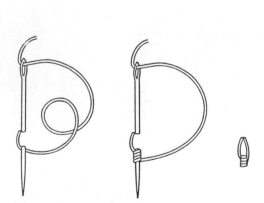

Lazy daisy bullion stitch

BULLION STITCH

This stitch should be worked with a straw or millinery needle. The small eye will allow the needle to pass easily through the wraps. The number of wraps should equal the length of the back stitch.

Commence as though to make a back stitch the required length for the bullion stitch. Bring the needle up at the starting point but do not pull through. Wrap the thread around the needle, in a clockwise direction, the required number of times. Do not wrap too tightly. Place your left thumb over the wraps, then pull the needle through the wraps. As you pull the thread up firmly, the bullion will turn back. Adjust the wraps if necessary. Insert the needle at the starting point and pull through to complete the bullion stitch.

LAZY DAISY BULLION STITCH

This stitch is a combination of lazy daisy and bullion stitches. It is useful for leaves and flower petals and gives an interesting texture. It should be worked with a straw needle.

Bring the needle through at the point where you wish to begin your stitch. Hold the thread below your work and insert the needle close to where the thread first emerged. Bring the needle out at the desired distance, as though you are making a small lazy daisy stitch, keeping the thread underneath. Do not pull the needle through at this stage. Wrap the thread around the needle three to five times (or desired number) in an anti-clockwise direction. Place your left thumb over the wraps, then pull the needle and the thread firmly through the wraps. To anchor the stitch insert the needle at the tip of the bullion and pull through to the back of the fabric. Pass on to the beginning of the next stitch. Be sure to work each stitch the same to ensure that the long stitch down the side lies on the same side.

Lazy daisy or detached chain

LAZY DAISY OR DETACHED CHAIN

This is a very useful stitch for leaves and flower petals.

Bring the needle through at the point where you wish to begin your stitch. Hold the thread below your work and insert the needle to the right, close to where the thread first emerged. Bring the needle out at the desired distance, keeping the thread underneath. Fasten the loop at the end with a small straight stitch. Pass on to the beginning of the next stitch.

DOUBLE LAZY DAISY STITCH

This stitch is useful for leaves and large flower petals. It can be worked in two colours.

The inside stitch is worked first as an ordinary lazy daisy stitch. The larger second stitch is worked outside and around the first stitch.

Double lazy daisy stitch

FLY STITCH

Fly stitch is an open lazy daisy stitch. The tying stitch can vary in length as required. It can be worked singly, vertically, horizontally or radiating into a circle.

Bring the thread through at the top left of your design line. Insert the needle a little distance away to the right and take a small diagonal stitch to the centre with the thread below the needle. Pull through and fasten with a straight downward stitch.

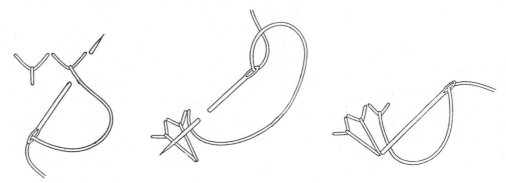

Fly stitch

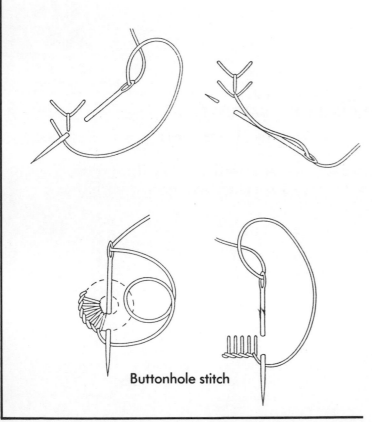

Buttonhole stitch

BUTTONHOLE STITCH

This stitch is the same as blanket stitch but the stitches are worked closer together. It can be worked in a row or a circle.

Start on the outside edge and work from left to right. Hold the thread below and take a downward straight stitch and draw up with the thread underneath the needle. Continue in this way, spacing stitches as required.

SATIN STITCH-SLANTED

This stitch should be worked with even stitches to cover the fabric completely, resulting in a smooth finish. Work with a stabbing motion for better tension. The use of a hoop will help.

A running stitch may be worked first to outline the design. This will help to form a good edge. Work slanting stitches closely together across the area outlined.

STRAIGHT STITCH

Straight stitch is a single satin stitch and can be worked in any direction and to any length. The use of a small embroidery hoop will help you achieve good tension. Do not make the stitches too long, as snagging may occur.

LONG AND SHORT SATIN STITCH

This stitch can be used to fill areas too large to be covered by satin stitch. It can also be used to achieve subtle shading. The use of a small embroidery hoop will help you achieve good tension.

Work the first row in alternate long and short satin stitches. Closely follow the outline of the design shape. The following rows are then worked in long stitches in a 'brick' fashion until the area is filled. The gaps in the final row will be filled with short stitches.

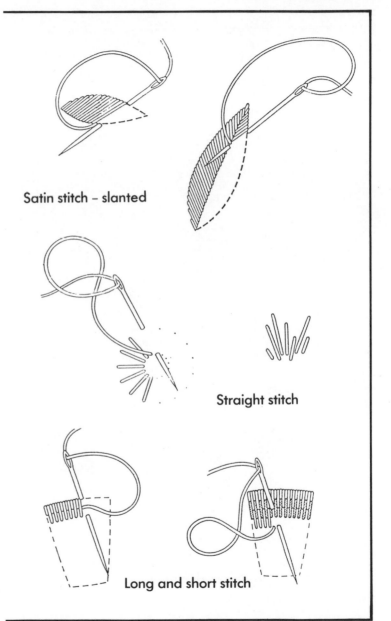

Satin stitch – slanted

Straight stitch

Long and short stitch

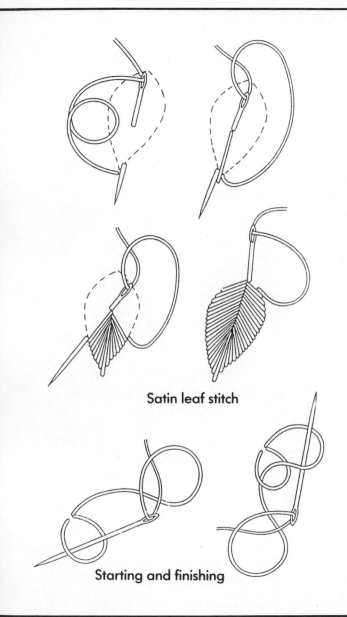

Satin leaf stitch

Starting and finishing

SATIN LEAF STITCH

This variation of satin stitch is easy to work and forms a very realistic leaf. It is taken from Brazilian embroidery.

The first stitch should be a little longer than you might expect, in order to form a good point on the leaf. Work the first satin stitch from the point of the leaf back into the centre of the leaf. Bring the needle back up on the right of the first stitch at the leaf tip. Take this second stitch back to the central leaf vein and insert the needle just below, but very close to the first stitch. Work the satin stitches alternately from each side, fanning them as the leaf forms. At the same time, continue to work closely down the central vein. You may need to add one or two extra stitches on one side of your leaf if it is not symmetrical.

STARTING AND FINISHING

The use of a small knot is quite an acceptable and secure way to begin your work.

There are many satisfactory ways to finish off your thread. The following method is used for smocking and is neat and secure.

Take a small stitch to form a loop. Pass the needle through the loop to form a second loop. Pass the needle through the second loop and pull up tightly to form a secure knot.

STITCH GLOSSARY (left-handed)

STEM OR OUTLINE STITCH

A simple stitch for stems, outlines and filling.

Working from right to left, take small, even straight or slightly slanting stitches along the design line. Leave a space between the point where the needle emerges and the previous stitch. Keep the thread below or on the same side of your work. For wide stem stitch, make the stitches on a greater angle.

Stem or outline stitch

WHIPPED STEM STITCH

Whipped stem stitch gives a corded effect.

Work a row of stem stitch along the design line and bring the needle to the top of your work. Work in the opposite direction to that of the stem stitch. With the blunt end of the needle whip back through each stem stitch, but not into the fabric.

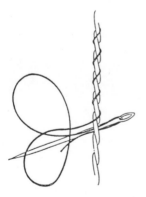

Whipped stem stitch

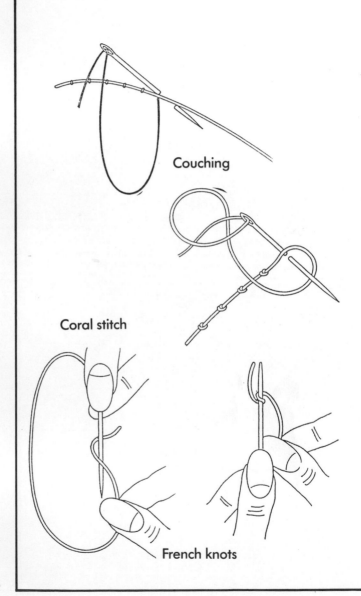

Couching

Coral stitch

French knots

COUCHING

The branches and flower stems in this book worked in couching have one or two strands of thread laid down and one strand for the tying stitch of matching thread. The use of a small hoop will help with tension. Use two needles and keep them on top of your work to prevent tangling. Anchor the thread not in use and keep it out of the way. Short stems in couching can be worked with one needle and thread.

Lay the thread along the design line, holding and guiding its direction with your thumb. Tie it down with small straight stitches made at regular intervals.

CORAL STITCH

Coral stitch is a simple knotted line stitch useful for flower stems.

Hold the thread to the right along the design line. Take a small stitch towards you with the thread over and around the needle; pull through forming a knot. Continue at regular intervals.

FRENCH KNOTS

When working French knots you will have more control and be able to develop a rhythm if a small (10 cm/4″) hoop is used. To increase the size of knots, use more strands of thread.

Bring the thread up at the desired spot. Hold the thread firmly with your right hand. With the needle pointing toward you, place it under the thread from the right-hand side and twist it around once. Insert the needle close to where the thread first emerged, but not in the same hole. Draw the thread around the needle to firm the knot and pull through to the back. Pass on to the position for the next knot.

FRENCH KNOT STALKS

French knot stalks are worked in the same manner as French knots. The use of a small embroidery hoop will help you achieve good tension.

To form the stalk, after encircling the needle with the thread, insert the needle the desired distance away from where it first emerged. Pull through to the back and pass on to the position for the next stitch.

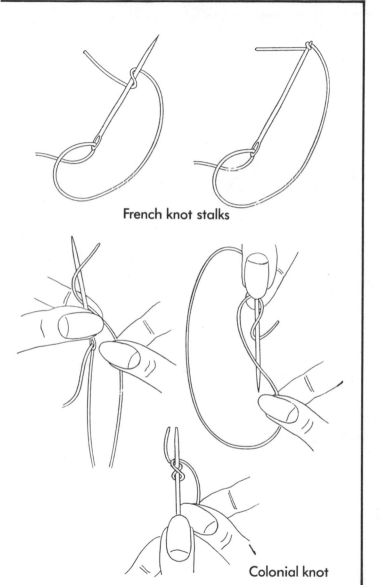

French knot stalks

COLONIAL KNOTS OR CANDLEWICKING KNOTS

This stitch differs from a French knot in that the twists are worked in a figure of eight. It stands up high on the fabric and needs to be worked very firmly. You will have more control and be able to develop a rhythm if a small (10 cm/4") hoop is used.

Bring the thread up at the desired spot. Hold the thread firmly with your right hand. With the needle pointing away from you, place it under the thread from the right-hand side and twist it in a clockwise direction away from you. The needle will now be facing you. The second part of the stitch is the same as a French knot. Now place the needle under the thread from the right-hand side and twist it around once back to the original position.

Insert the needle close to where the thread first emerged, but not in the same hole. Draw the thread around the shaft of the needle to firm the knot and pull through to the back. Pass on to the position for the next knot.

Colonial knot

BULLION STITCH

This stitch should be worked with a straw or millinery needle. The small eye will allow the needle to pass easily through the wraps. The number of wraps should equal the length of the back stitch.

Commence as though to make a back stitch the required length for the bullion stitch. Bring the needle up at the starting point but do not pull through. Wrap the thread around the needle, in an anti-clockwise direction, the required number of times. Do not wrap too tightly. Place your right thumb over the wraps, then pull the needle through the wraps. As you pull the thread up firmly, the bullion will turn back. Adjust the wraps if necessary. Insert the needle at the starting point and pull through to complete the bullion stitch.

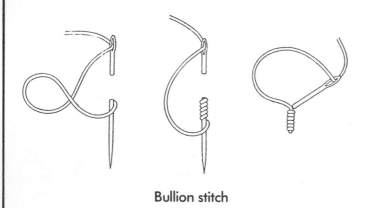

Bullion stitch

LAZY DAISY BULLION STITCH

This stitch is a combination of lazy daisy and bullion stitches. It is useful for leaves and flower petals and gives an interesting texture. It should be worked with a straw needle.

Bring the needle through at the point where you wish to begin your stitch. Hold the thread below your work and insert the needle close to where the thread first emerged. Bring the needle out at the desired distance, as though you are making a small lazy daisy stitch, keeping the thread underneath. Do not pull the needle through at this stage. Wrap the thread around the needle three to five times (or desired number) in a clockwise direction. Place your right thumb over the wraps, then pull the needle and the thread firmly through the wraps. To anchor the stitch insert the needle at the tip of the bullion and pull through to the back of the fabric. Pass on to the beginning of the next stitch. Be sure to work each stitch the same to ensure that the long stitch down the side lies on the same side.

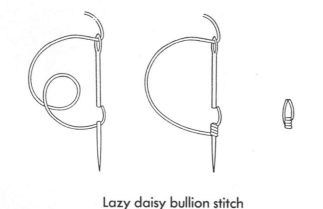

Lazy daisy bullion stitch

LAZY DAISY OR DETACHED CHAIN

This is a very useful stitch for leaves and flower petals.

Bring the needle through at the point where you wish to begin your stitch. Hold the thread below your work and insert the needle to the left, close to where the thread first emerged. Bring the needle out at the desired distance, keeping the thread underneath. Fasten the loop at the end with a small straight stitch. Pass on to the beginning of the next stitch.

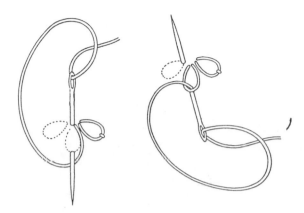

Lazy daisy or detached chain

DOUBLE LAZY DAISY STITCH

This stitch is useful for leaves and large flower petals. It can be worked in two colours.

The inside stitch is worked first as an ordinary lazy daisy stitch. The larger second stitch is worked outside and around the first stitch.

Double lazy daisy stitch

FLY STITCH

Fly stitch is an open lazy daisy stitch. The tying stitch can vary in length as required. It can be worked singly, vertically, horizontally or radiating into a circle.

Bring the thread through at the top right of your design line. Insert the needle a little distance away to the left and take a small diagonal stitch to the centre with the thread below the needle. Pull through and fasten with a straight downward stitch.

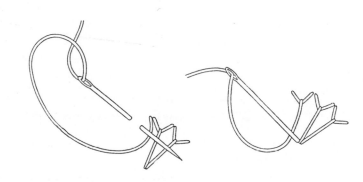

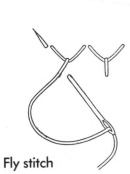

Fly stitch

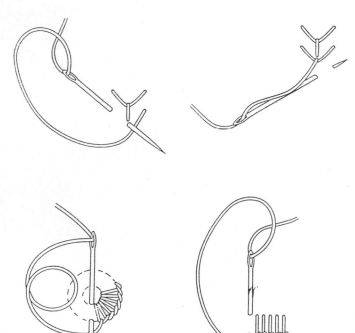

Buttonhole stitch

BUTTONHOLE STITCH

This stitch is the same as blanket stitch but the stitches are worked closer together. It can be worked in a row or a circle.

Start on the outside edge and work from right to left. Hold the thread below and take a downward straight stitch and draw up with the thread underneath the needle. Continue in this way, spacing stitches as required.

SATIN STITCH-SLANTED

This stitch should be worked with even stitches to cover the fabric completely, resulting in a smooth finish. Work with a stabbing motion for better tension. The use of a hoop will help.

A running stitch may be worked first to outline the design. This will help to form a good edge. Work slanting stitches closely together across the area outlined.

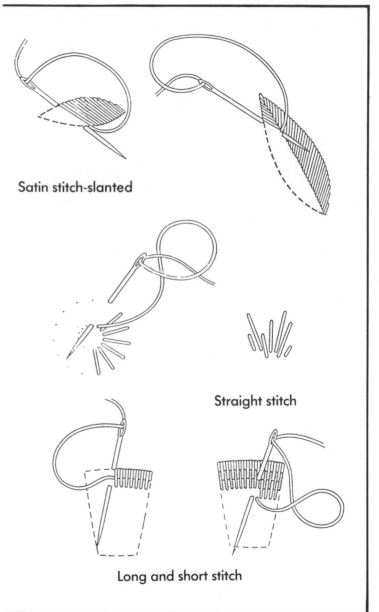

Satin stitch-slanted

STRAIGHT STITCH

Straight stitch is a single satin stitch and can be worked in any direction and to any length. The use of a small embroidery hoop will help you achieve good tension. Do not make the stitches too long, as snagging may occur.

Straight stitch

LONG AND SHORT SATIN STITCH

This stitch can be used to fill areas too large to be covered by satin stitch. It can also be used to achieve subtle shading. The use of a small embroidery hoop will help you achieve good tension.

Work the first row in alternate long and short satin stitches. Closely follow the outline of the design shape. The following rows are then worked in long stitches in a 'brick' fashion until the area is filled. The gaps in the final row will be filled with short stitches.

Long and short stitch

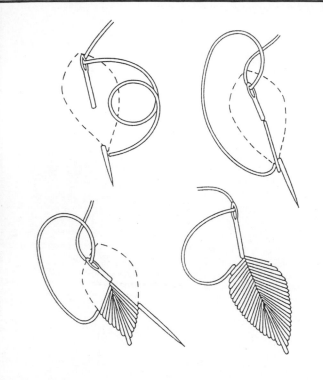

Satin leaf stitch

SATIN LEAF STITCH

This variation of satin stitch is easy to work and forms a very realistic leaf. It is taken from Brazilian embroidery.

The first stitch should be a little longer than you might expect, in order to form a good point on the leaf. Work the first satin stitch from the point of the leaf back into the centre of the leaf. Bring the needle back up on the left of the first stitch at the leaf tip. Take this second stitch back to the central leaf vein and insert the needle just below, but very close to the first stitch. Work the satin stitches alternately from each side, fanning them as the leaf forms. At the same time, continue to work closely down the central vein. You may need to add one or two extra stitches on one side of your leaf if it is not symmetrical.

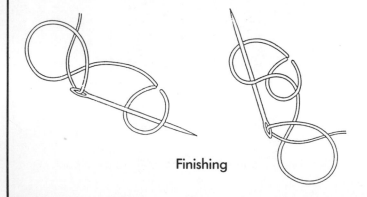

Finishing

STARTING AND FINISHING

The use of a small knot is quite an acceptable and secure way to begin your work.

There are many satisfactory ways to finish off your thread. The following method is used for smocking and is neat and secure.

Take a small stitch to form a loop. Pass the needle through the loop to form a second loop. Pass the needle through the second loop and pull up tightly to form a secure knot.

APPENDIX A
THE FRAMING OF NEEDLEWORK

There are probably as many ways to frame a piece of needlework as there are ways to furnish a room in which the needlework will hang. While most will look attractive, few will be done correctly, and this will be revealed over a period of time.

The most important thing to remember in framing needlework, as indeed in framing any original artwork, is that the nature of the work should not be materially altered during the framing process. In the case of recently completed needlework of the size referred to in this book, this means that, before the embroidery is placed in the frame, it should be laced over archivally sound board in the manner illustrated (see illustration 1). This will keep it firm and straight inside the frame.

It should not be glued down with wet glue or dry mounted in a heat press. Both these methods will cause the fabric to discolour and hasten its deterioration. Neither is it recommended that needlework be stapled on to a backing board or kept in position with masking tape.

Many embroiderers prefer to do the lacing of the work themselves. It is not difficult, merely time-consuming and, therefore, expensive if a professional carries out the operation. Care must be taken to ensure that the weave of the fabric is straight and that the embroidery remains clean. Remember that grease transferred from hands to the surface of the fabric may not show up immediately, but will become apparent in time. Your picture framer should be able to supply you with the correct grade of card on which to lace the embroidery. Having laced the needlework on to its backing, it is ready for framing.

Decisions will now have to be made on what sort of frame best suits the embroidery, whether or not it should be placed behind glass, and if it should be 'matted' with a cardboard surround. These are not only

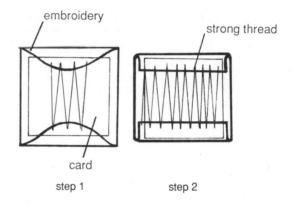

embroidery

strong thread

card

step 1   step 2

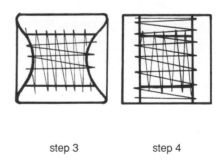

step 3   step 4

Illustration 1: lacing an embroidery — from the back

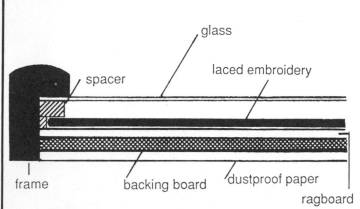

Illustration 2: framing without a matt — side view

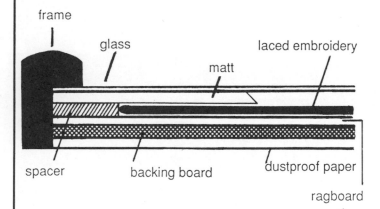

Illustration 3: framing with a matt — side view

aesthetic considerations but also very practical ones.

On cottage embroidery, simple wooden frames, with maybe just a hint of colour along the inside edge, work best. More complicated frames, particularly gilt ones, tend to overwhelm the needlework. Whatever frame is chosen, it should be deep enough and strong enough to accommodate the embroidery, the glass, the backing and any other materials used.

As a general rule, embroideries are best put behind glass. Glazing keeps the dust off, prevents them becoming dirty, and will help keep the silverfish out. However, when the work is glazed, care should be taken that the glass does not touch the surface of the embroidery: moisture condensing on the inside of the glass can migrate into the fabric and cause the fibres to deteriorate. Glass can be kept away from the embroidery either with a small spacer placed between the glass and the embroidery, underneath the rebate of the frame (see illustration 2), or by using a single or double matt (see illustration 3), or a combination of spacer and matt if the surface of the embroidery is raised.

Because the needlework and the glass are separated, non-glare or non-reflective glass should not be used. Most non-glare glass when used in this way blurs the image and dulls the colours. Clear glass is required or, if the embroidery is to hang in a very brightly lit area, a Plexiglas which inhibits the passage of ultra-violet light should be considered.

Except on samplers, matting is recommended as it is not only practical but also serves a very important aesthetic function. An archivally sound, coloured matt (green is often used when the image contains flowers) will not only enhance the image but also prevent the frame from visually crowding the embroidery. Remember that matts look better if they are large – at least five centimetres (2 inches) wide, with the bottom of the matt, slightly larger than the top and the sides, say six or seven centimetres (2½-3 inches). Any smaller than this and the matt and frame may look like concentric, coloured rectangles around the image, and the whole effect will be spoiled.

It is important that the card on which the embroidery is laced, and that used for the matting and backing of the embroidery, is archivally sound. Normal wood-pulp card is not archivally sound. It contains acidic materials which will eventually mark the embroidery.

Finally, when the embroidery is placed in the frame, the frame should be sealed with a good quality tape (not masking tape as it deteriorates too quickly) or completely papered over. This will prevent any dust or insect life entering the frame from the back.

If you adhere to these basic principles this should ensure the long life of the embroidery.

Ross Henty
Canberra Art Framing Company

APPENDIX B
DMC STRANDED COTTON AND
COLOUR NAMES IN NUMERICAL ORDER

white	blanc neige	316	antique mauve — medium
ecru		317	pewter grey
208	lavender — very dark	318	steel grey — light
209	lavender — dark	319	pistachio green — very dark
210	lavender — medium	320	pistachio green — medium
211	lavender — light	321	Christmas red
221	shell pink — very dark	322	navy blue — very light
223	shell pink — light	326	rose — very deep
224	shell pink — very light	327	violet — very dark
225	shell pink — ultra very light	333	blue violet — very dark
300	mahogany — very dark	334	baby blue — medium
301	mahogany — medium	335	rose
304	Christmas red — medium	336	navy blue
307	lemon	340	blue violet — medium
309	rose — deep	341	blue violet — light
310	black	347	salmon — very dark
311	navy blue — medium	349	coral — dark
312	navy blue — light	350	coral — medium
315	antique mauve — very dark	351	coral

352	coral — light	498	Christmas red — dark	605	cranberry — very light
353	peach flesh	500	blue green — very dark	606	bright orange-red
355	terracotta — dark	501	blue green — dark	608	bright orange
356	terracotta — medium	502	blue green	610	drab brown — very dark
367	pistachio green — dark	503	blue green — medium	611	drab brown — dark
368	pistachio green — light	504	blue green — light	612	drab brown — medium
369	pistachio green — very light	517	wedgwood — medium	613	drab brown — light
370	mustard — medium	518	wedgwood — light	632	negro flesh — medium
371	mustard	519	sky blue	640	beige grey — very dark
372	mustard — light	520	fern green — dark	642	beige grey — dark
400	mahogany — dark	522	fern green	644	beige grey — medium
402	mahogany — very light	523	fern green — light	645	beaver grey — very dark
407	sportsman flesh — dark	524	fern green — very light	646	beaver grey — dark
413	pewter grey — dark	535	ash grey — very light	647	beaver grey — medium
414	steel grey — dark	543	beige brown — ultra very light	648	beaver grey — light
415	pearl grey	550	violet — very dark	566	Christmas red — bright
420	hazelnut brown — dark	552	violet — medium	676	old gold — light
422	hazelnut brown — light	553	violet	677	old gold — very light
433	brown — medium	554	violet — light	680	old gold — dark
434	brown — light	561	jade — very dark	699	Christmas green
435	brown — very light	562	jade — medium	700	Christmas green — bright
436	tan	563	jade — light	701	Christmas green — light
437	tan — light	564	jade — very light	702	kelly green
444	lemon — dark	580	moss green — dark	703	chartreuse
445	lemon — light	581	moss green	704	chartreuse — bright
451	shell grey — dark	597	turquoise	712	cream
452	shell grey — medium	598	turquoise — light	718	plum
453	shell grey — light	600	cranberrry — very dark	720	orange spice — dark
469	avocado green	601	cranberry — dark	721	orange spice — medium
470	avocado green — light	602	cranberry — medium	722	orange spice — light
471	avocado green — very light	603	cranberry	725	topaz
472	avocado green — ultra light	604	cranberry — light	726	topaz — light

727	topaz — very light	793	cornflower blue — medium	838	beige brown — very dark
729	old gold — medium	794	cornflower blue — light	839	beige brown — dark
730	olive green — very dark	796	royal blue — dark	840	beige brown — medium
731	olive green — dark	797	royal blue	841	beige brown — light
732	olive green	798	delft — dark	842	beige brown — very light
733	olive green — medium	799	delft — medium	844	beaver grey — ultra dark
734	olive green — light	800	delft — pale	869	hazelnut brown — very dark
738	tan — very light	801	coffee brown — dark	890	pistachio green — ultra dark
739	tan — ultra very light	806	peacock blue — dark	891	carnation — dark
740	tangerine	807	peacock blue	892	carnation — medium
741	tangerine — medium	809	delft	893	carnation — light
742	tangerine — light	813	blue — light	894	carnation — very light
743	yellow — medium	814	garnet — dark	895	hunter green — very dark
744	yellow — pale	815	garnet — medium	898	coffee brown — very dark
745	yellow — light pale	816	garnet	899	rose — medium
746	off white	817	coral red — very dark	900	burnt orange — dark
747	sky blue — very light	818	baby pink	902	garnet — very dark
754	peach flesh — light	819	baby pink — light	904	parrot green — very dark
758	terracotta — very light	820	royal blue — very dark	905	parrot green — dark
760	salmon	822	beige grey — light	906	parrot green — medium
761	salmon — light	823	navy blue — dark	907	parrot green — light
762	pearl grey — very light	824	blue — very dark	909	emerald green — very dark
772	yellow green — very light	825	blue — dark	910	emerald green — dark
775	baby blue — very light	826	blue — medium	911	emerald green — medium
776	pink — medium	827	blue — very light	912	emerald green — light
778	antique mauve — very light	828	blue — ultra very light	913	Nile green — medium
780	topaz — ultra very dark	829	golden olive — very dark	915	plum — dark
781	topaz — very dark	830	golden olive — dark	917	plum — medium
782	topaz — dark	831	golden olive — medium	918	red copper — dark
783	topaz — medium	832	golden olive	919	red copper
791	cornflower blue — very dark	833	golden olive — light	920	copper — medium
792	cornflower blue — dark	834	golden olive — very light	921	copper

922	copper — light	970	pumpkin — light	3052	green grey — medium
924	grey green — very dark	971	pumpkin	3053	green grey
926	grey green — medium	972	canary — deep	3064	sportsman flesh — very dark
927	grey green — light	973	canary — bright	3072	beaver grey — very light
928	grey green — very light	975	golden brown — dark	3078	golden yellow — very light
930	antique blue — dark	976	golden brown — medium	3325	baby blue — light
931	antique blue — medium	977	golden brown — light	3326	rose — light
932	antique blue — light	986	forest green — very dark	3328	salmon — dark
934	black avocado green	987	forest green — dark	3340	apricot — medium
935	avocado green — dark	988	forest green — medium	3341	apricot
936	avocado green — very dark	989	forest green	3345	hunter green — dark
937	avocado green — medium	991	aquamarine — dark	3346	hunter green
938	coffee brown — ultra dark	992	aquamarine	3347	yellow green — medium
939	navy blue — very dark	993	aquamarine — light	3348	yellow green — light
943	aquamarine — medium	995	electric blue — dark	3350	dusty rose — ultra dark
945	sportsman flesh — medium	996	electric blue — medium	3354	dusty rose — light
946	burnt orange — medium	3011	khaki green — dark	3362	pine green — dark
947	burnt orange	3012	khaki green — medium	3363	pine green — medium
948	peach flesh — very light	3013	khaki green — light	3364	pine green
950	sportsman flesh	3021	brown grey — very dark	3371	black brown
951	sportsman flesh — very light	3022	brown grey — medium	3607	plum — light
954	Nile green	3023	brown grey — light	3608	plum — very light
955	Nile green — light	3024	brown grey — very light	3609	plum — ultra light
956	geranium	3031	mocha brown — very dark	3685	mauve — dark
957	geranium — pale	3032	mocha brown — medium	3687	mauve
958	seagreen — dark	3033	mocha brown — very light	3688	mauve — medium
959	seagreen — medium	3041	antique violet — medium	3689	mauve — light
961	dusty rose — dark	3042	antique violet — light	3705	melon — dark
962	dusty rose — medium	3045	yellow beige — dark	3706	melon — medium
963	dusty rose — ultra very light	3046	yellow beige — medium	3708	melon — light
964	seagreen — light	3047	yellow beige — light	3712	salmon — medium
966	baby green — medium	3051	green grey — dark	3713	salmon — very light

3716	dusty rose — very light	3761	sky blue — very light
3721	shell pink — dark	3765	peacock blue — very dark
3722	shell pink — medium	3766	peacock blue — light
3726	antique mauve — dark	3768	grey green — dark
3727	antique mauve — light	3770	flesh — very light
3731	dusty rose — very dark	3772	negro flesh
3733	dusty rose	3773	sportsman flesh — medium
3740	antique violet — dark	3774	sportsman flesh — very light
3743	antique violet — very light	3776	mahogany — light
3746	blue violet — dark	3777	terracotta — very dark
3747	blue violet — very light	3778	terracotta — light
3750	antique blue — very dark	3779	terracotta — ultra very light
3752	antique blue — very light	3781	mocha brown — dark
3753	antique blue — ultra very light	3782	mocha brown — light
3755	baby blue	3787	brown grey — dark
3756	baby blue — ultra very light	3790	beige grey — ultra dark
3760	wedgwood — light	3799	pewter grey — very dark

INDEX

FLOWER GLOSSARY